CROSSING THE THRESHOLD; EMBRACING THE CALL

CONCEPTUALIZING, CO-CREATING AND BUILDING COMMUNITY THROUGH RITES OF PASSAGE

KAMAU PTAH

wordeee
where words connect

CROSSING THE THRESHOLD; EMBRACING THE CALL

CONCEPTUALIZING, CO-CREATING AND BUILDING COMMUNITY THROUGH RITES OF PASSAGE

Non-Fiction
Crossing the Threshold; Embracing the Call:
Conceptualizing, Co-Creating and Building Community Through Rites of Passage

ISBN: 978-1-959811-58-9 (Paperback)
ISBN: 978-1-959811-59-6 (e-book)

Library of Congress Control Number: 2024911918

Cover Design: Awan Design
Interior Design: Amit Dey
Author Cover Photograph: Matthew Morgan/Supreme Shotz
Other photo credits, Jamaica Jackson, photography page, 142 Matthew Fuego, pages 40, 100, 113 and Matthew Morgan/ Supreme Shotz, page, 256

Published by Wordeee in the United States, Beacon, New York 2024

Website: www.wordeee.com
X Formerly Twitter: wordeeeupdates
Facebook: facebook.com/wordeee/
e-mail: contact@wordeee.com

Crossing the Threshold is an introspective masterpiece. Kamau takes the reader on an evolutionary journey shaped by the concept of Sankofa. Relying on the wisdom of the ancestors, the book details the roots of Kamau's call and his drive to step into his purpose without hesitation or concern for what the voices of his day would say. Kamau's love and compassion for this work is unrivaled and in my opinion, it transcends the landscape of youth work of today.

—*Leonard Gerard Townes, Commissioner*
Westchester County Department of Social Services

From vulnerable narratives internalized as sacred stages to his own manhood, Kamau Ptah translates an introspective reflection of life into a brilliant pedagogy that calls each reader to consider their own personal stories and locate their own initiating steps to adulthood. Further, Ptah provides a *Blackprint* workbook to coordinating Rites of Passages for the "called" and "chosen" who are inspired and primed by the reading of *Crossing the Threshold; Embracing the Call, Conceptualizing, Co-Creating and Building Community Through Rites of Passage*.

—*Dr. R.A. Ptahsen-Shabazz*
Author, Blacktotheroots.net

Crossing the Threshold; Embracing the Call: Conceptualizing, Co-Creating and Building Community Through Rites of Passage will provide the reader a clear and present avenue to personal transformation and self-healing.

It will also serve as the catalyst to a broader and deeper healing for those who are so moved to answer their call to facilitate and lead a broader and deeper community transformation through the Rites of Passage process. Kamau Tehuti Ptah, through his personal deep reflective and active personal transformation has powerfully articulated the blueprint steps to follow. It is a must and critically important read!

—*Ron Walker*
Founding Executive Director
Coalition of Schools Educating Boys of Color

I am thrilled to bear witness to the magic and inspiration formed into this manuscript turned into a full book by my Djembe Djedna-Brother from another Mother! Kamau Ptah & I have walked many of life path's together; sometimes at different times but only to meet each other in the right time and space to lead and grow. I have had the blessing to gleam from his work, growth, and mastery in leading young Black & Brown boys into Manhood and leadership. This book is a brilliant facilitation into the reality of his own personal journey that has brought him through many of life trials that he now has masterfully crafted into a Living Word, a Living Book to help guide, heal, and instruct generations to come. To come back into the majesty of Ourselves....Our true Afrikan Selves with Love for ourselves, our mothers & fathers, our daughters & wives, Love our Sons/Suns, Brothers & Others, to the liberation and victory of what it is To Be African. To a Black Man - Authentically & in MA'AT!

SO! I give you the Akoben Enterprises call:

"SHARPEN YOUR EYES! TUNE YOUR EARS! SO YOU KNOW WHAT YOU SEE. UNDERSTAND WHAT YOU HEAR.

MINUTE BY MINUTE, HOUR BY HOUR!

AS WE KNOW OUR STORY WE KNOW OUR POWER!"

"AKOBEN!!"

"READY FOR ACTION!!"

—*Baba Kojo Ayinde Johnson*
Musician, Entrepreneur, Instructor, Author

Crossing the Threshold is a deeply profound, courageous, and prophetic memoir chronicling Kamau Ptah's life and legacy. This biographical sketch explores Kamau's journey to understanding the complexities of Black manhood in America and his unyielding quest to define his life's journey. A must-read for those committed to understanding the transformational power of ideas in shaping our destiny!

—*David C. Miller, PhD*
Dare To Be King Project, LLC
Author, Dare To Be King: What If the Prince Lives?

If I stop to say "WOW!" every few minutes while reading, I know I have been deeply moved by the prose, mesmerized by the scenarios, and motivated to keep reading more. A longtime admirer of my colleague, Kamau Ptah, I am grateful for this poignant autobiographical overview shining light on his ability to use his wisdom to guide others. I loved Kamau like a mom before, and now, even more so after the privilege of gaining a deeper glimpse into his heart, mind, and soul.

—*Dr. Deidre R. Farmbry*
Educational Consultant and Friend of COSEBOC
(The Coalition of Schools Educating Boys of Color)

With his new book, *Crossing the Threshold*, Kamau Ptah has provided readers an extraordinary gift. This insightful and deeply personal narrative of his journey and experience in coming to understand who he is in the world, is one that will benefit many youth today. For Black young men in particular who are bombarded with conflicting and contradictory messages about what it means to be a man today, this book can serve as a source of grounding and as a guide on how to live a purposeful and fulfilling life. Written with elegance and insight, *Crossing the Threshold* is truly a treatise. Full of wisdom and thought provoking ideas, it will open eyes and hearts to the possibilities that await those who seek to understand who they are and why they are here.

—*Pedro A. Noguera, PhD*
Dean, Rossier School of Education
Distinguished Professor of Education
University of Southern California

Crossing the Threshold; Embracing the Call: Conceptualizing, Co-Creating, and Building Community Through Rites of Passage by Kamau Ptah is a powerful testament to the transformative potential of rites of passage. With clarity and honesty, Ptah navigates the complex terrain of identity and truth, offering readers a sense of safety and guidance. Through the lens of conceptualization and community building, Ptah's work inspires individuals to embark on a journey of self-discovery and collective healing.

—*Harvey Hinton III, Ph.D.*
Founder/Chief Change Agent Kuumba, LLC

Crossing the Threshold; Embracing the Call is a gateway and guide for those seeking a part of themselves they have never seen or experienced before. Ptah, is a journeyman who embraces the hills and valleys of growth and transformation as a Black man navigating a world that doesn't always see and accept his power, purpose and humanity. This book is a must read for every person who identifies as a member of the African Diaspora. It is an invitation to restore, reseed and remember the essence of who we are as a people and to realign ourselves with the "Source" of our power and authority as melanated masters of our own destinies.

—*Shawnee Benton Gibson, LMSW/FDLC*
CEO, Spirit of a Woman, LLC
Co-Founder, The ARIAH Foundation

CONTENTS

TRIBUTE AND DEDICATION

To my mother, Dawn Patricia Patterson, for her unwavering love, guidance, devotion, support, and presence during my major passages in life.

Love Supreme!

FOREWORD

t is with great pleasure that I write the Foreword to *Crossing the Threshold; Embracing the Call: Conceptualizing, Co-Creating and Building Community Through Rites of Passage* by Kamau Ptah. The reason it is a pleasure is because I have seen first-hand the deep impact that Kamau has had on thousands of students in his work over the decades.

The oldest word in human history relative to teaching is *Seba*. In the ancient Kemetic (Egyptian) language of *Medu Netcher (hieroglyphics)*, it has three primary meanings: "teach," "door" and "star." This, along with other data, tells us that the ancient African philosophy of education is, "The Teacher opens the door to the Universe so that the Student may shine like a star" (Akua, 2022). A *Seba* is a Master Teacher.

For decades, Kamau Ptah has been opening the door to the Universe and helping students shine like a star in some of the most challenging schools and communities through his teaching, leadership and curriculum development.

I have often said, "Those who think our children can't be reached have never seen a Master Teacher teach." Kamau Ptah is just that kind of teacher. Now, through *Crossing the Threshold*, he opens a treasure chest of practical, philosophical and pedagogical, tools to transform African American youth and youth of color.

Black youth and youth of color have been gangsterized, criminalized, adultified and hyper-sexualized through skillful media manipulation and miseducation. As a result, the problem is made to seem intractable.

One of the great tragedies in American education is that most teachers have never been under the guidance of a Master Teacher and most leaders have never been under the guidance of a Master Administrator. Kamau Ptah is both.

In America, we are at an impasse in education. As a nation, America is no longer sustainable with such large numbers of African American students and students of color in underserved, under-funded, culturally irrelevant schools and classrooms.

For those that are serious about education, whether public, private or charter, Kamau Ptah's methods and outcomes need to be studied and implemented. Schools of Education in colleges and universities would do well to do the same with pre-service teachers and leaders. Then, and only then, can our children cross the threshold to greatness.

—Chike Akua, PhD
Associate Professor, Department of Educational Leadership
Clark Atlanta University
Author, Education for Transformation:
The Keys to Releasing the Genius of African American Students

ABOUT THIS BOOK

Crossing the Threshold; Embracing the Call: Conceptualizing, Co-Creating and Building Community Through Rites of Passage is a representation of a lifelong journey of my passages, coupled with over thirty years of professional experiences of conceptualizing, designing, implementing, co-creating, and facilitating rites of passages in every community I have been blessed to serve.

This book was written for you and your community. It has been developed with the wisdom of many. My hope is that it will be used to build this generation and many future generations. It will serve as a guide to identify the pillars and key components for designing the rites of passage that capture the pulse of your community's needs and the outcomes anticipated upon the successful passage of our boys, young men, and the highest aspirations of our community.

You can write and make notes in this book. However, we suggest you consider writing your thoughts and answers in a journal, notebook or create a file on your computer. As your knowledge base expands and your community's needs evolve, you'll want to update your entries.

Within this book you'll see various symbols utilized as design elements. Below is a reference guide to symbols and their meaning:

Akoben:

The word Akoben literally describes a horn that was blown by Ashantis to summon warriors, alert people, and prepare for battle. Origin: The word is derived from the term aben and it means animal horn. Spiritual meaning: Akoben symbolizes devotion, loyalty and service.

Sankofa (1):

The word Sankofa is from the Asante Twi language of the Akan people of Western Africa, which we now know as Ghana and the Ivory Coast. The word itself means, "to return and get it."

The most prominent of the Asante Adinkra symbols for the concept of Sankofa depicts a mythical bird about to take flight with its head turned backwards. The egg in its mouth represents the 'gems' or knowledge of the past upon which wisdom is based; it also signifies the generation to come that would benefit from that wisdom.

Sankofa (2):

The word Sankofa is from the Asante Twi language of the Akan people of Western Africa, which we now know as Ghana and the Ivory Coast. The word itself means, "to return and get it."

This symbol means "Return and Take" representing the importance of remembering and learning from the past to build the future. "Learn from your past."

Sesa Wo Suban:

Sesa Wo Suban (se-sa wo su-ban) symbol means "Change your character." It signifies personal reflection and transformation. It's a composition of two symbols; the inner star which represents a new day and an outer wheel which implies initiative and moving forward. The symbol encourages people, especially youth, to make a positive change to the world by their actions.

Gye Nyame:

Meaning "except for God," symbolizes God's omnipotence through the knowledge that people should not fear anything except for God. Another interpretation of "except for God" is that no one has seen the beginning of all creations, nor will anyone live to see the end, except for God.

SANKOFA REFLECTIONS: AN INTRODUCTION

My name is Kamau Tehuti Ptah. The name Kamau derives from the Kikuyu language and is spoken by the Kikuyu people of Kenya belonging to the Bantu ethnic nation who traveled from the Congo region. The name was gifted to a cluster of young men who went through initiation training together. The group was called Rika. The initiation process required training, guidance, counseling and circumcision from the elders and rites facilitators to help usher in the transition from boyhood to manhood. The young men in the group would embrace their initiation group's name as a given name (Rika ria Rika) as a form of association, but would also keep their original name. Thus, the man's name at birth might be Kenyatta, but he might choose to use his Rika name, Kamau. As a result, men usually had two or three names (birth name, initiation name, and nickname). The name Kamau is also represented in the language of Kiswahili from the Swahili people of East Africa. In Kikuyu and Kiswahili, Kamau means the Silent Warrior. Tehuti and Ptah are Kemetic Spiritual archetypes that reflect the pantheon of Divine powers that make up the cosmology of Ancient Nile Valley Spiritual and cultural ethos. Tehuti means Divine articulation through oral and written communication. Tehuti is the personification of wisdom conveyed through thought, speech, and action. Ptah is the architect of creation. He is the creative faculty that inspires and influences the creative process. He is the *spark* of creation and maker of all living things in the Universe. He is often associated with craftsmen and metal workers.

1

Kamau Tehuti Ptah translates to mean the Silent Warrior who articulates the Creator's masterful design through Divine thoughts, words, and actions. Wow! What a powerful title for a man to uphold. The path that I have chosen in this journey requires a name that reminds me to maintain a strong alignment with the Infinite powers and possibilities of the Creator's Omnipresence. With this name it charges me to make myself available to be a vessel for the highest possibilities and intentions for the Divine expression of the sacred, profane, and mundane aspects of my journey.

Kamau Tehuti Ptah was not my name at birth. On August 26, 1969, I made my entrance to the planet as Mark Elliot Patterson. My mother named me after one of her favorite soap opera characters during this time. Prior to changing my name, I met with both of my parents separately and shared my decision and rationale for the change. To my surprise, my mother not only supported my decision, but she also encouraged me as she acknowledged the name change as an exercise in self-determination. My father was a different story. He listened attentively, heard my explanation, and comprehended my reasoning, yet bluntly stated, "I will never call you that name. It's not the name we gave you." I knew at that moment I would have to be intentional about not allowing his decision to create a wedge in our relationship. I grappled with the question, how close can I really be with anyone who doesn't' acknowledge and honor my transformation? I wanted both my parents to validate and affirm my decision. As a son, I enjoyed making my parents proud, however with this decision it was bigger than my preferences and my desire to please them. I was driven by a higher call: the Spirit's directive to align with a sacred vibration that would be a constant reminder of my nature and my mission. This change would also be a definitive demarcation from the frequency of the enslaver's name and energy, a result from my Ancestors being violently branded as property to serve someone else's vision and legacy.

As I stood in line at the Manhattan Civil Courthouse at 111 Centre Street, there was a knowingness and certainty that guided each step I took even with the great appeal from the persona of Mark that was making the last plea to sprint off the line and forget that I ever heard the name Kamau. Once I filed my documents and walked out of the civil court, there was a renewal of my Spirit and a freedom that I felt; still at the same time I felt sadness, as Mark Elliot Patterson was a good guy as well. Under that name there were many fond memories and relationships that were established. I chalked it up as my journey had already been written. Mark Elliot Patterson was the essential seed that gave birth to Kamau Tehuti Ptah.

I never particularly cared for my birth name. It never quite captured the essence of who I really was. I thought that it was plain, and it lacked the creative spark that was necessary to articulate my Soul's intelligence. It felt imbalanced, as if I gave more energy to the name than the name furnished me. I didn't hate the name, yet it felt like I needed to identify with a sound frequency that was satisfying and uplifting to my Spirit. However, as fate would have it, my mother *was* in the ballpark with the essence of my energy, as Mark is a Roman God of war. The warrior intention charged me with the assignment, and my name conversion to Kamau aligned me with a cultural and Spiritual connection that was satisfying to my Soul's desire.

Elliot, my middle name derives from the Hebrew language. It means the "Lord is my God." Again, my mother was on to something, yet I don't think she was fully aware of the meaning of the name(s) she chose for me. Still as the Almighty would have it, there was a harmonious alignment with the name that I chose for myself.

My surname at birth was Patterson. Patterson has its origins in Scotland, Ireland, and Northern England. The name means "son of Patrick." The last name Patterson was more than likely the name of my Ancestor's enslavers who would brand their "property" and claim ownership of the enslaved African and Indigenous people. The original names of our Ancestors were stripped away during the enslavement and colonization process. The intention of the name removal was to eradicate all memories of the traditional sacred name that carried powerful meanings, which connected us to our lineages, legacies, and Divine assignments. It was this narrative that created the rationale for changing my name. I embraced the idea that I could never realize true freedom carrying the names of the enslavers and oppressors of my Ancestors. I, like some of my contemporaries entering adulthood that were deeply influenced by African-centered philosophy, took on new names that had African, Islamic, Hebrew, and Indigenous origins.

I began referring to myself as Kamau around 1990. My cultural and historical knowledge was rapidly increasing, and my identity was being transformed. At this stage of life, my daily mission was fueled by the "Know Thyself" edict and the way that I viewed myself and the world through emerging Afrocentric eyes. My circles of influence and obligation were all reflections of my expanding consciousness of being a child of African Ancestry. These belief systems were represented in my daily rituals, routines, and norms. As a student at Hampton University, much of my academic and extra-curricular focus was centered on building and expanding on my thirst to fill the void of my self-concept and self-worth through knowing my cultural and historical narrative and charging myself to live up to the standards of excellence that my Ancestors modelled. I made it my personal commitment to live up to these pillars by embodying what I interpreted as obligations to honor my Ancestor's genius, wisdom, values, struggles and victories. I charged myself to fully activate the mandates of Black Excellence and Sankofa Power:

> A return to one's origin that is rooted in the values, practices, rituals, and intelligences that help activate a memory of a healthy identity and instills the responsibility of continuing a legacy of excellence.

> (Ptah, COSEBOC DRUM Professional Learning definition).

My time and energy during my freshman and sophomore years at Hampton were devoted to building a new organization. The African Studies Cluster was created to help harvest the brilliance within the student body at Hampton. Through rituals, reflection, self-examination, and study we were committed to healing the identities of children of African Ancestry who were miseducated about our heritage and culture. At the core of our mission, we were working to heal the wounds that were inflicted through abusive White Supremacy culture and institutional racism, which permeated the worlds in which we were educated and socialized. We were curating a necessary educational healing space for what Dr. Joy Leary DeGruy, and other African-centered scholars would diagnose as Post Traumatic Slave Syndrome, which is:

> A theory that explains the etiology of many of the adaptive survival behaviors in African American communities throughout the United States and the Diaspora. It is a condition that exists because of multigenerational oppression of Africans and their descendants resulting from centuries of chattel slavery–a form of slavery which was predicated on the belief that African Americans were inherently/genetically inferior to whites. This was then followed by institutionalized racism which continues to perpetuate injury, thus resulting in **M.A. P.**:

- **M**: Multigenerational trauma together with continued oppression
- **A**: Absence of opportunity to heal or access the benefits available in the society; leading to
- **P**: Post-Traumatic Slave Syndrome (DeGruy,www.joydegruy.com)

On my visit home from Hampton, I increased my "Know Thyself" activity by attending the powerful lecture series at the First World Alliance in Harlem and The Slave Theatre in Brooklyn. As my Winter and Spring breaks were different from the City College of New York's vacation, it afforded me the opportunity to attend classes with my girlfriend at the time, who was a Black Studies and Psychology major. During these sessions, I had the opportunity to sit in classes with the erudite warrior educators of this era who were leading the movement of African-centered philosophy, education, and research. I was blessed to sit in classes with Dr. Leonard Jefferies, Dr. Jeanie Bains, Dr. John Henrick Clarke, and Professor James Small. Additionally, I would frequent Muhammad's Mosque #7 in Harlem, the Bereshith Cultural Institute in Mount Vernon (where the African Hebrew Israelite services would occur on the Shabat), and the Asr and Ast Society in Brooklyn. These spaces served as water holes for the activation of the intelligences and sensibilities that supported me with remembering who I am and nurturing what would become the essential ingredients of my mission. As I was experiencing a radical change in how I viewed myself, I heard the call and felt the aggressive nudge to change my name.

As I viewed books and inquired about the names that I heard in the African-centered circles, I remember the sensation that I felt in my body when I heard the name Kamau. The energetic resonance generated a certain sense of peace, safety, and remembrance. When I researched the meaning and learned that it meant *silent warrior*, I knew that I would walk with this name in some form or fashion as it aligned with my Spirit and how I moved throughout life. As I pondered, meditated, and reasoned on the name, my girlfriend at the time affirmed, "Kamau, that is perfect! That is who you are." It was during this time that I embraced the first name and began to refer to myself as Kamau. The name was also assigned to me through the brotherhood that I became an honorary member of, as part of the African Studies Cluster. The name of the fraternity was Kemet Nu. In cultural circles, where I spent much of my time, I began to introduce and refer to myself as Kamau or Brother Kamau. It wasn't until 2004 that I decided to legally change my name.

These Are My Roots

I embrace the Spiritual notion and belief that originates in Indigenous and Aboriginal cultures, which avows that when a Spirit enters the physical realm it chooses the parents for life's great adventure. With this intention, I chose my parents, Dawn Patricia Burrowes Patterson and Frank Julian Patterson, Jr.

My mother was born in 1946 in Kingston, Jamaica and migrated to the United States in 1958 at twelve years of age. She is an only child and was referred to affectionately by her mother as "One Chicken." According to my mother, she vowed that when she became a mother, she would have more than one child. As the youngest of two siblings, my birth was planned with the intention of creating a healthy family dynamic with my brother and my parents. There was great excitement and anticipation of my arrival and my mom looked forward to welcoming me and introducing me to my brother. According to my mother, my birth was much more challenging than my brother's, which she described as "easy and quick." My birth, on the other hand, was quite different. My mom shared that I hung on to her back for hours! However, when I finally arrived there was no thought of pain, and as my mom tells it, "He was a joy to behold! I claimed him immediately, as he looked just like me."

At the time of my arrival the country was still in a state of shock after the assassination of Dr. Martin Luther King, Jr. James Earl Ray pled guilty to his murder and was sentenced to ninety-nine years in prison. The year 1969 was chaotic with the Vietnam War televised and the activists protesting. Demonstrators numbering 250,000 marched on Washington against the Vietnam War. Additionally, the newly elected 37th President Richard Nixon implemented the removal of the first U.S. troops from South Vietnam in Saigon. In the world of the arts, Lorraine Hansberry's play *To Be Young, Gifted, and Black* premiered in New York City. In sports, the New York Jets won Super Bowl III, defeating the Baltimore Colts. It is their last championship to date.

The year 1969 also witnessed Black student organizations on college campuses (i.e., Cornell University, Duke, North Carolina A&T) throughout America facilitate student rallies, protests and takeovers of administrative buildings demanding Black Studies and addressing concerns of lack of opportunities for students and faculty of African ancestry. Moreover, 1969 celebrated New York Representative Shirley

Chisolm as the first Black woman elected to Congress. She would later be one of the founders of the Congressional Black Caucus and Women's Caucus. Lastly, I can't forget about one of the most momentous events that played a huge role in the culture of children in my generation with the debut of *Sesame Street* on National Education Television, the predecessor of the Public Broadcasting Service (PBS).

Upon my arrival home from Misericordia Hospital
to my loving family. Bronx, NY, 1969

As a child, my mother lived in Harlem with my grandmother, Joyce Gloria Taylor Burrowes (affectionately known as Nana). Nana possessed a vivacious and flamboyant personality. In New York City, she pursued a career as a medical and psychiatric health provider. In her personal life, she was the life of the party. She loved tasty food, good drinks (spirits), jokes, laughter, and controversy. She was colorful in her dress, speech, and daily life routines. The only time when Nana was calm was when she was knitting and crocheting; even during these activities she would polyrhythmically tap her foot and chew gum with pops every third to fourth chomp. Nana's claim to fame was her beautiful Afghan blankets, love for music, and her incredible culinary skills, particularly dishes from sweet Jamaica. How blessed I was to come home from school to the aromas of oxtail, rice and peas, cabbage, or escovitch snapper, dumplings, bananas, plantains, and other traditional Jamaican cuisines. Nana had a deep love for family and was always eager to share vibrant stories about our family and heritage. She was adept at the art and science of assessing character and would always find an appropriate creative nickname for her loved ones who she always showered with extreme generosity.

As my Nana lived out loud, my mother represented the complete opposite character. Growing up, my mother was overwhelmed by Nana's extroverted and sometimes vulgar behavior. Her boisterous energy was unpredictable, and one never knew what she might say or do in public. Nana genuinely didn't give two "flying farts" about what anyone thought about her. If she heard music that moved her spirit, she would "wine her battam to deh floor." She was unapologetic about who she was. She had the attitude that conveyed, "all who nuh like it, bite it."

My mother was extremely uncomfortable and utterly embarrassed by Nana's antics, so much so that her persona was much more reserved and socially appropriate. Unless, of course, she was angered. My mom has always been a dignified woman. She radiates timeless beauty, stateliness, and pride. She possesses an inner beauty of compassion, love, and joy. These qualities are experienced through her interior design, cooking, and her ability to find humor and express uncontrollable gut-busting laughter at the simplest things, particularly her ability to laugh at herself. When I hear her laugh, it translates to victory as my mom endured difficult ordeals to earn the joy and freedom that she enjoys today.

My mother was a substance abuse counselor. She responded to this call as a loving assignment to comprehend and help my father overcome his alcoholism. In her career, her mission was to support her clients with their journey to sobriety. Her assignment was not easy as she had to guide people to and through their thresholds and have them confront the deep wounds and shadows that they had avoided, neglected, or attempted to escape. This process required my mother to constantly be self-reflective and dance with her own shadows to be effective. She was and continues to be on a path towards healing, transformation, and personal growth.

My mom earned her stripes and persevered through the classic and tumultuous mother-daughter trials, the heartbreak and betrayal of infidelity and divorce, Nana transitioning to become an Ancestor (gratefully after healing their wounds), and not believing that she had identified a clear purpose in her life. From a 'rites of passage' initiation viewpoint, I have witnessed my mother voluntarily respond to calls that have challenged her to the core. These trials charged her to look deep within and embrace vulnerability in ways that were *sheroic* examples of warriorship. I know that she would not recognize her strength in this manner, yet I have been blessed to ride in the front seat of her life and witness her confront her shyness and social awkwardness by putting herself in situations where she had to speak publicly. I remember her joining theatre productions and challenging herself to embrace the discomfort of performing live. I have observed her overcome her deep fear of water and become a lifelong student of swimming. I have witnessed her persistence through the excruciating heartache of divorce and the self-determining drive to restore a sense of personal mission in life. I have observed my mom build and repair the relationship with my Nana and her father.

My maternal grandfather, Roy Kenneth Burrowes (born 1926) also hailed from Kingston, Jamaica. My grandfather was a jazz musician who left Jamaica in the 1940s to pursue his aspirations to be a part of this incredible artistic movement that was bustling in the United States, particularly in New York City. His decision to follow his dreams, earned him great notoriety as a Jamaican Hall of Fame Jazz Artist who played with legends like Duke Ellington, Sonny Rollins, Max Roach, Abby Lincoln, Count Bassie, Clifford Jordan, Sun Ra, Ray Charles, to name a few. However, his musical successes did not come without the nightmare of what was internalized by my mother as abandonment. My mother did not meet her father until she moved to the United States. My grandfather, warmly known as "Bubbles," was a brilliant artist who devoted his life to music. As many musicians find it difficult to find balance between their craft and other life functions, Bubbles at times had his blinders on where nothing else mattered but his musical pursuits. Additionally, there were periods of what all struggling artists go through with maintaining regular jobs while pursuing their passions. Bubbles' creative talents and artistic regiment compromised his ability to be family-oriented and I am sure that my mom felt a sense of rejection from Bubbles' absence. I can also empathize with the internal pain that Bubbles must have felt with pursing his calling and sacrificing family conventions.

I have watched my mother continue to show up to "the calls," sometimes disguised as traumas in her life, and courageously press on and radically grow through the "trials by fire" and "dark nights of the soul." Her life journey prepared her to be present with me during the most challenging and traumatic life initiations that I have experienced. Her ability to hold space and process the major lessons have been invaluable to my transformations and journey to adulthood.

The greatest lesson that I have learned from my mother is that the only way out is to go through. She modelled how to meet and accept where you are in life and be present, authentic, and committed to change, particularly when life is summoning for a change in basic assumptions. I have also learned from her to appreciate the arts, cultural aesthetics, and travel. My mother continues to pursue the path of a lifelong learner and she always moves with grace, elegance, impeccable order, harmony, and joyful laughter.

My maternal grandparents, Roy "Bubbles" Burrowes and Joyce Taylor Burrowes
Kingston, Jamaica

Father of Mine

My father was a proud son of Harlem, New York City. He was born on August 18, 1941, to the late Marie Margaret Taylor Patterson (born 1920) and Frank Patterson, Sr. (born 1918). My grandmother's hometown was Caroline County, Virginia and my grandfather was born in Harlem, yet his parents were from Charleston, South Carolina. My paternal grandparents were a part of the great migration era, which was the movement of people of African Ancestry out of the Southern United States to the Northeast, Midwest, and West from 1915 to 1970. During the 20th century, this mass Southern departure of six million people transformed the appearance and culture of America.

My grandmother, lovingly known as Grandma, was the family *Djeli (griot,* storyteller, keeper of the family narratives) and possessed the gift of storytelling. At family reunions, Grandma would connect the dots and bring to life the Ancestors whose names and narratives were shared in a humorous and dignified manner. She had a powerful mastery of words and was an exceptional communicator. She was an avid reader and was deeply enthusiastic about learning. She particularly enjoyed crossword puzzles, autobiographies and books related to history and politics. Like Nana, Grandma loved knitting and crocheting, especially for her grandchildren. My paternal grandmother was a "Stay at Home Mom" and was the primary caretaker of her four children, although I do recall hearing that at one time in her life, she worked at the New York Public Library. Grandma was extremely nurturing and personified unconditional love for our entire family, particularly her grandchildren.

My grandfather, lovingly known as Grandpa, was known as "The Rock" of our family. He was the embodiment of pride and was deeply devoted to family. He was quick witted and enjoyed competitive banter with anyone who thought they had a fast mind and verbal dexterity. Grandpa's warm smile lit up any room with his glow of confidence and charming presence. He was always impeccably dressed and would sport a stylish hat to complement any outfit that he wore. As a child, I would spend hours in his closet trying on all the hats he possessed.

Grandpa was a decorated and celebrated Supervisory Inspector in the United States Customs Bureau. He was one of the organizers of the American Federation of Government Employees in Customs and was its first Vice President. He was also a founding member of the US Customs Sentinel Society, a group of men of African and Indigenous Ancestry devoted to ensuring a pipeline of qualified Black Indigenous candidates for careers in customs.

Grandpa was a man of his era, where there existed extraordinarily few opportunities to unmask and be vulnerable. With the pressures of navigating manhood during the 1930s and 40s, a man of African and Indigenous Ancestry would mentally and emotionally put on the armor of invincibility and rarely show signs of what might be perceived as weakness. For men of this time, there were limited ways of expressing emotions that reflect the full range of the human experience. The suppression of fear, pain, trauma, confusion, sadness, and other human feelings was the norm, as men would be judged harshly for openly acknowledging these feelings publicly and in many cases even privately. Men of African and Indigenous Ancestry often projected pride, confidence, and a cool exterior that would be the mask that was permanently worn to counter or disguise the emotional taboos that would translate to being soft or weak. Verbal expressions of love, intimacy, and compassion were often filtered through an attachment to a delivery that was appropriate for a man to express, which would often come off distant, vague, or harsh to the uninitiated receiver.

There was no doubt in my mind and heart that my grandfather loved me, yet the formality of his communication created a barrier for the full expression of his heart. I recall for the first twelve years of my life (except for my infant and toddler years) that my grandfather would greet me and my brother with handshakes when we visited as opposed to hugs. This was common as I don't remember experiencing hugs from too many men during my formative years of my maturation. I first experienced masculine affection through hugs at the Hebrew Israelite Temple, where there was a ritual handshake that would involve an embrace of the right forearm and a shoulder-to-shoulder connection performed three times starting from the left shoulder to the right and back to the left. Sometimes depending on the relationship, the last embrace would be completed with a kiss on the cheek. I remember my brother and I began to embrace my grandfather with hugs during my *tween* phase and my brother's early teens. I recall my grandfather's awkwardness about this manner of greeting and how his body would be a little tense. Though reluctant at first, there was also an acceptance of the invitation for him to convey something that his heart yearned to communicate that only a hug can express. It felt like it was something that he didn't know the value of, yet once he experienced it, he fully embraced the opportunity to connect with his grandsons in a way that none of us ever imagined was possible. As a child there was nothing more affirming than bonding with an esteemed elder through the powerful medicine of a hug. From that first hug, the greeting and departure ritual was practiced every time we visited my grandfather. I still feel a sense of covering and connection when I reflect on these sacred embraces with my grandfather. I wished that my father could've experienced this type of warmth from his dad, yet, just as we initiated my grandfather, my brother and I also invited my father to experience the power of hugs.

My father had an interesting duality that made his character unique. In one instant he could be calm, reserved, unassuming and quiet and in another moment, he was the life of the party and extremely extroverted. Though he was reserved, he enjoyed being social, particularly at festive events. He had a great love for sports (track and field, boxing, football, and basketball) and music (jazz, soul, R&B, calypso, and reggae). His albums were his treasured possessions, which he cared for like they were vintage instruments or classic cars. In my father's early adult years, he embarked on a career of civic service by running for a public official seat in the Bronx and he later served in the Army National Guard. His strong inclination and sensibility for justice guided him to work for the US Department of Housing and Urban Development (HUD). One of the highlights of his career was when he served as a primary investigator in a major case that brought Brooklyn's Starrett City into equal opportunity compliance.

As a dad, my father was a grounding presence for my brother and me. One principle that he emphasized and desired for us to internalize was the concept of true brotherhood and friendship. It was his greatest charge for us to build a strong bond as siblings. His driving motivation for ensuring that my brother and I were connected was the distance that grew between my father and his brother. I don't know all the details that created the separation, yet I do recall my father sharing with me that when he returned home from college, friends in the neighborhood informed him that his brother was an active user of heroine. My father expressed his initial denial and disbelief, yet when he addressed his brother, he was devastated to learn that the rumors were true. My father carried a burden of guilt. He felt he could have somehow prevented my uncle from making destructive choices if he had invested more in their relationship. It was a silent guilt that he walked with daily. This was the driving force that made him so determined to ensure that my brother and I were connected. His intentions were realized as my brother and I are deeply connected as siblings and friends.

My father's leadership was a distinctive combination of authoritative and restorative. His vocation's standard, which was centered on equity, was also practiced in our home. He embraced the same philosophy as the great boxing referee, Mills Lane, who would always affirm in his instructions before champion fights, "I'm firm, yet I'm fair." There were bottom line expectations for chores, academics, and general character virtues that demanded respect. These ideals were not preached, yet they were modelled in his daily actions. My father's easy-going manner enabled him to approach awkward conversations with a sense of candor and grace. He possessed the temperament and Spirit of an advisor and counselor. His quiet nature was magnetic and inviting to many who found comfort in his grounding presence. Our home was a hub, particularly for his friends to come have a "taste" of their preferred spirits (alcoholic drink). With the consumption of the truth serum, accompanied by jazz, R&B or whatever the vibe musically called for, it was an invitation for the men to purge their blocked thoughts and emotions. As I secretly listened in on these sessions, I was intrigued by the vulnerability that occurred and the different dimensions of men's complex issues. I witnessed these men peel back the armor of their social and professional masks and bare their Souls. It was the first time that I witnessed men cry and bring language to the pain, shame, and traumas that they were experiencing. I don't think my father was aware that he created a healing space for his comrades. He missed his true calling as a counselor or an advisor. I am sure that some aspects lived in his career as an investigator, yet his persona seemed perfectly fitting for a restorative counseling practitioner.

Additionally, a few of my friends and older guys from my community would share that they had quality conversations or "Real Talks" with my father, usually centered on making healthy choices or overcoming obstacles. I was always proud to learn that my father inspired the older neighborhood guys who were usually the leaders in the community. These were not formalized sessions; most times they were impromptu moments that were generated by the young men's inquiry, a preventative approach to signs that were revealing a risk, or a response to a behavior that was potentially destructive.

There were times during my teenage years, particularly my sophomore and junior years of high school, where my father would enter my room during my late-night studies. At this phase of my life, I really began to own my academic journey and would burn the midnight oil studying and working on assignments. My father would unexpectedly come into the room with a sense of urgency, which was different from his normal temperament. His energy wasn't aggressive, yet it carried the feeling of a high priority. He would instruct me to stop working and say, "You *gonna* have to get a C on tomorrow's project." It was during these moments that he would want to share aspects of his narrative and discuss deep matters of the heart. It was in these moments that I would provide for him the same sounding board role that he would play for his close brethren, where I would listen without judgment and hold space for his heart-centered reflections. These conversations mostly occurred after my father had had a few drinks and desired to reflect on his life. It was during these father-to-son moments that I learned about the childhood joys and pains that my father stored in his heart and mind. He would reflect on playing with army soldiers with his brother, going to Star Lake Sleep Away Camp, and his summer employment as a Park Attendant. He would also share some of his painful memories and disappointments, particularly the hurt that he experienced with my grandfather. He shared memories about how he longed for my grandfather to come to his track meets, yet he was unable to due to his active work schedule. He also expressed a memory about a time when my grandfather taught one of his best friends how to drive before receiving his own lessons. I observed how much pain my father felt by what he internalized as disloyalty. During these sessions it was inevitable for him to mention the heartache and powerlessness that he felt about his brother's addiction.

In addition to these reflective memories, my father would also share his philosophies and Spiritual beliefs. Though he was not "religious," he would make it a point of emphasis to affirm the reality of God by identifying miracles that could not be explained by scientific methods. He would say, "Mark, ask your science teacher tomorrow, if there is no such power as God, how does milk get into a woman's breast for the mother to be able to feed her child?" Most significantly for me during these moments were the times when my father verbalized that he loved me. I used to resent that he would mostly convey these words when he was intoxicated, yet I grew to realize that men of preceding times were not raised with an emotional intelligence and vocabulary. The sentiments were more expressed through the acts of service. I acknowledged, appreciated, and valued all forms of love from my father and grandfathers. In hindsight, I truly cherish these memories and recognize that I received *wholistic* narratives about my father's perspective on our past, present, and visions for the future.

From the affirmative stories to the trauma, I recognized that it all helped to inform me about our collective journey that birthed the gifts, qualities and enlightenment that has shaped my calling.

As destiny would have it, who knew that I would concoct my mother's vocation and altruistic healing intentions and my father's unconventional restorative sensibilities and translate that into the work that I am engaged in as an educator, rites of passage facilitator, healing aspirant, and a student practitioner of Indigenous Spiritual Technologies.

My paternal grandparents, Frank Patterson, Sr. and Marie Patterson,
with my father, Frank Patterson, Jr.
Harlem, NYC, 1942

Brothers Gonna Work It Out

As previously mentioned, my mother being an only child, truly desired for my older brother to have a sibling to experience life with and create a strong bond. Rodney Anthony Patterson (Dr. R. A. Ptahsen-Shabazz) was born March 7, 1966. He is my elder by three years. The earliest family narrative of what I now view as an initiation into brotherhood was when I was a newborn just arriving home. It is said that my brother's excitement to meet me was abruptly halted when he held me for the first time, and I vomited in his face. My purging and his being able to hold space for my release is a symbolic representation of our initiations that would occur throughout the various stages of our journey in life together.

My brother was Divinely assigned to be my first rites of passage peer facilitator, charged with the responsibility of preparing me for the tumultuous world of childhood from a youngster's perspective. The first lesson that I clearly needed to know was he was my elder and that the very nature of my existence was to be company and cast for his life productions. Thankfully, I am grateful my parents were present to guide and teach the true virtue and meaning of brotherhood.

From early on Rod was exceptional in most areas that he put his time, energy, and effort towards. He was blessed with a self-determining drive that needed no external validation for approval. His decisions were independent and influenced by his own voice and intentions. He also always possessed a strong will and devotion to excellence. Whatever the endeavor, be it academics, athletics, the arts or everyday mundane activities, Rod embraced early in life a high-performance standard for himself.

Academics always came easy for my brother. He always received excellent grades and would consistently make the Honor Roll. As I was a mediocre student at best, my parents would have to lift my spirits and comfort me during report card season. They would explain to me that my brother was gifted and that his intellect was an exceptional quality, that I should not compare myself to him. To ensure that my intellectual

19

esteem wasn't completely shattered, my parents showed me their report cards, where their grades were more aligned with my average and occasionally slightly above average marks.

As a method for supporting my academic development, my parents thought it was a promising idea for my brother to tutor and assist me with homework assignments, yet that turned out to be disastrous as my slow and methodical processing was painstakingly grueling for my brother's impatience and what he thought were his best strategies to assist with my assignments. The tutoring sessions would always abruptly end with him saying, "Mom, I tried! I can't do this anymore." It was a relief to me, as it was difficult to open myself to learning with my insecurities combined with his lack of patience.

From childhood, my brother always had a deep passion for teaching, particularly when it came to the identity of people of African Ancestry. At around thirteen years of age, he fell in love with Bob Marley and the message of freedom, redemption, cultural pride, and self-determination. His obsession with the message and the music would have him play Bob Marley from sunrise to sunset. I remember my paternal grandfather spending the day with my brother and upon dropping him back home he shared, "I listened to so much reggae today that I grew dreadlocks" as he pointed to his bald head. As Marley's music was contagious and we all were subject to the 24/7 marathon mixes, I found myself wanting to dig deeper into the message and at times when I was home alone, I would pull out his albums and listen while reading the lyrics. One day when I was enjoying my private listening session, my brother excitedly interrupted my vibes and said, "You don't know what he's saying" and proceeded to read the lyrics and break down every message in the song. After that experience, every time I heard my brother nearby or approaching the space of my Marley sessions, I would quickly put on my Yellow Man 45 records to avoid the Marley lecture. These were the beginnings of my brother's professorship and path to earning his Ph.D. in Africana studies. These early moments were the seeds to the authoring of his book, *Black to the Roots: Reggae's Rise, Downpression, and Reascension.*

The greatest validation that a younger sibling seeks is to be affirmed by their older siblings. There is an air of confidence that is internalized when one is acknowledged for their efforts and achievements. In my brother's daily pursuits, he personifies confidence. He is often distinguished by the glide in his stride and the rhythm of his walk. He has always moved with a grace and nobility that conveys a purpose driven path. I always admired his ability to blaze his own self-determined direction and rarely did he fall victim to the negative influences of peer pressure. As a role model, he set the example for how to be your authentic self. Through observing him navigate youth culture in the 70s and 80s, I knew that I didn't have to abandon my values and compromise myself for the approval of others. His voice and presence were genuinely him and his mistakes were choices that he made from his own self-determining decisions.

As mentioned, my first initiations (life tests and challenges) were facilitated by my brother. Card games, Monopoly, Chutes and Ladders, Backgammon, Chinese Checkers and Othello were all fun games that bring joy, comradery and excitement. Well, playing any game with my highly competitive brother was like going to war. Like all wars and battles, it starts with destroying the psyche of your opponent. My brother would play these games with a relentless mission to annihilate your mind. He didn't just like to win the game, he relished seeing you crack, punished, and demoralized. These games brought out a monstrous side of him. A sinister energy that yearned to assert a power that would completely leave you depleted of the joyful intention of playing the game. There were times where these games ended in a physical fight or with me throwing the game or cards in a state of frustration and rage. I just never understood why we couldn't play these games without the torture. Even when my friends would come over and play Monopoly, they were traumatized not only for going bankrupt, but also for the psychological abuse and energy depletion caused by the mean-spirited style of play and the unique rules that were added to the game to place more pressure on the players. For example, when we played Monopoly at my house, my brother added a rule where if you didn't close the deal on the property, you landed on by saying, "Buying" or "I'm Buying" before the next player rolled the dice, you wouldn't own that property even if you paid for it. In other words, you would lose your money if someone rolled the dice, and you didn't claim the property by saying "Buying." After a six-hour marathon of Monopoly, my friends would be in tears ready to return home at 3:00 a.m..

Other initiations came in the classic big brother bullying fashion that would always have me questioning myself, "Why?" Why did he lock me in the dark basement or the back porch? Why did he leave me dangling from the top of the swings when my shorts got stuck to the metal on the bar? Why couldn't I accompany him with his friends to the basketball game? Why was he allowing his friends to roast me and make me the butt of their jokes? Why did he show me where the Christmas gifts were hidden and tell me that there is no Santa Claus?

There is no way that I would have chosen these experiences at this stage of my life as a preference to engage with my big brother. However, like all initiations, there were valuable and indelible lessons that I received from these trials that were essential for my growth. My brother was consciously or unconsciously preparing me to navigate male youth culture in the 70s and 80s. These trials that I endured gave me the ability to identify and activate the warrior protector of self. Not only was I prepared physically to defend myself, but I also learned the psychological tactics of intimidation, which served me well in my encounter with children in my community, school, and other spaces that I navigated where there was no adult supervision. If it were not for these challenges my brother put me through, my kindhearted nature would have positioned me to be prey for the vulturous bullies and wanna be bullies in my community. My brother's unrelenting taunts helped me to locate and channel the aggression that's necessary for when people don't respect your boundaries and are determined to disrupt your peace. Though I preferred not to unleash this aggression, I knew if needed, I would be able to channel and direct it to keep myself and loved ones safe.

The athletic initiation was a path that also called for this assertive energy to be conveyed in a healthy manner. My brother's competitiveness found maximum expression in athletics as he ran track, played football, and basketball. Nevertheless, track was our first love and primary sport/passage. Through our early exposure to track and field, we were immersed into a culture that functions with its unique lexicon, norms, routines, and practices. Though this chapter was not introduced as a formal initiation, track was our first passage, and it always presented the mirror to examine who we were from practice to practice and meet to meet. Every time one lines up on the track, they are not only competing against other competitors, but they are also competing against themselves and the stopwatch that is recording the truth of how you prepare for each call to improve yourself via the times you run. As an athlete in any sport, the ritual of getting in the zone and summoning the courage to confront fear and experience pain are the trials that are ubiquitous in athletics.

My brother excelled in track as it was the perfect sport that channeled his competitive nature and ambitious standards for performance, which was a reciprocal function for his approach to the sport. As with any endeavor, once my brother chooses the path, he commits himself to excellence. It was through track that I observed and learned from my brother how to cultivate the mindset and the discipline that it takes to become an elite athlete, which is transferable to any life pursuit. Early workouts before school regardless of the weather, mirror shadowing to work on his technique, writing affirmations on all his school notebooks that read "Rod, the Track Star," running hills until nauseated and vomiting, viewing VHS track meets and studying *Track and Field news* were all a part of the daily regimen of my brother's life from age seven until twenty-two. For many of those years, I also honed my warrior mindset as we would train together and build a powerful bond through the discipline of track. In the sport, my brother didn't taunt and bully as much. That expression was quelled as the virtue of sportsmanship was learned and became a value in the culture of the sport. Professorship qualities were present as he would always be willing to teach a technical aspect of the sport or approaches to inspire a champion's mentality. Track provided us both mirrors and lenses as we really became more acquainted with each other's heart, Spirit, and will through the preparation for events that were calling for peak performances. Through our track initiation a deeper love and mutual respect was enhanced as we were each other's greatest fans. Through the rituals, trials, enlightenment, and celebrations we experienced together, a brotherhood was strengthened on and off the track. These lessons would create indelible memories and transferable skills that would continue to be a part of our journeys, long after our track careers.

Another significant passage that was essential in the shared initiation with my brother was our "Know Thyself" path. As mentioned, the genesis of our cultural awakening was omnipresent in the music played in our house, as well as the cultural artifacts displayed in the interior design where our eyes could not help but consume a painting, mask, or symbol that reflected African and African Diaspora culture. From the sounds, images, and the literature that was present, the subconscious mind soaked up all the messages centered on cultural identity.

As children of the era of Black Power and the Civil Rights Movement, our parents were not "Race" people, yet they lived the Black experience with awareness of our collective identity, which represented our joys, accomplishments, struggles, and pains. As popular culture was and continues to be influenced by Black culture, we received powerful messaging from the presence and voices of John Carlos, Tommie Smith, Muhammad Ali, Kareem Abdul Jabbar, Jim Brown, James Earl Jones, Sidney Portier, Bill Cosby, Shirley Chisolm, Angela Davis, Maya Angelou, Nina Simone, Cicely Tyson, Don Cornelius, The Jackson 5, Bob Marley and the Wailers, Lord Kitchener, The Mighty Sparrow, Babatunde Olatunji, John Coltrane, Art Blakey, Gil Noble and a host of other influential voices of that era. As children we heard the frequent messaging that "Black is Beautiful," and "You have to work twice as hard" to be equal in a racist society. Songs like *Say It Loud, I'm Black and I'm Proud* and *To Be Young, Gifted and Black* were classics that continued to be revived through the early to mid-70s and helped shape our perspectives of what it meant to be children of African Ancestry in America. Though we were receiving these powerful and affirmative social messages through daily cultural experiences, we were introduced to formal religious rites through the Catholic Church. My brother and I were baptized as Christians under the Catholic denomination, and there we experienced our First Communion rites and ceremony. We were both being prepared for our Confirmation rites until my mom had a big argument with a Nun who refused to let my brother participate in the Confirmation because he missed some days of religious instruction to attend major track meets. This confrontation resulted in our departure from the church and the Catholic religion. I was grateful for the outcomes of this incident as I never felt connected to the Eurocentric doctrine or the majority Italian and Irish Church community. Honestly, the cultural style of the services felt Soulless, and I didn't feel the Divine presence in the experience. I remember having to really force myself to engage and invoke feelings for the "White" Jesus image that was always being portrayed as a victim. During the religious instruction classes, there were times that I thought that lightning would strike the classroom when some of the Italian boys would angrily make comments related to the "turn the cheek" ideology and refer to Jesus as a "faggot." I felt relieved and grateful not to have to return to that church again.

About a year later, we were introduced to another formal religious experience that was enlightening and transformative. My mother worked at the Mount Vernon Neighborhood Health Center in Mount Vernon, NY and became friends with a cultural custodian, community educator, Spiritualist, and keeper of sacred traditions. Baba Abishai Ben Rueben is a notable Baba (Cultural leader and Fictive father) in the Mount Vernon community, who has devoted his life to creating communities that are filled with the African and Indigenous ways of knowing and being. He is a drummer, educator, and a cultural practitioner throughout the New York Metropolitan area and beyond. It was Baba Abishai who invited Rod and me to the Bereshith Cultural Institute's Hebrew Israelite Shabat service. It was the response to this call that ignited the indwelling flames, accelerated our learning, and provided the essential tools to navigate our sacred Know Thyself paths.

I recall entering Bereshith and noticing the beautiful murals of images that displayed ancient noble, wise, and majestic men and women adorned in elaborate cultural attire that reflected the Divinity of life in Africa and ancient lands where our people dwelled. I also remember the warm Hebrew greeting of *Shalom* and *Shalom aleichem* (Peace be upon you) by the spirited men and women that were a part of the community. The service began with songs and drumming that activated memories that felt familiar. I was most impressed when I heard Priest Nasi lead the invocation in the Hebrew tongue. The ancient language, Priest Nasi's cadence and texture of his Spirit filled voice began to unlock feelings of remembrance and activate sensibilities that I never knew existed. I had never heard or experienced a prayer that was delivered in this manner. The ambience that was created by the drums, songs, and prayers was captivating. This, along with the frankincense and myrrh fragrances cleansed the air and contributed to the creation of a Spiritual vortex that welcomed The Most High and Ancestors into what felt like a timeless dimension. After the opening ritual was complete, the Spiritual leader, Kohain Nathania Ha-Levi presided over the service with an eloquent Divine Authority that I never witnessed in my Spiritual journey up to this phase of my life. His facilitation was effortless and very personalized. Though it was a formal facilitation, there were opportunities to engage and ask questions. It felt like a combination of a sermon, a Spiritual Council meeting, and a classroom all in one setting. Upon the completion of the service, food was served, and a protocol was adhered to where the elders received their meals first, the children and then the adults. The fellowship was genuine where the conversations flowed with ease and comfort. Though this was our first time, we were treated as family members. This experience was enlightening not just because of the powerful Spiritual message, for up to this phase of my life, I had never experienced this level of community bonding in my Spiritual and educational journey. Although we never formally joined or became Hebrew Israelites, my brother and I are still welcomed as family and connected to this community to this very day.

Another chapter in our Spiritual passages occurred when my brother returned from college (The University of South Carolina) on one of his breaks. His college studies and continuation of his Know

Thyself path were continuing to unfold. During his visit, he returned home with a VHS recording of the Honorable Minister Louis Farrakhan and invited the family to view it together. I was familiar with Minister Farrakhan as he made big news when he came to Madison Square Garden in 1985, in his quest to restore to life the Nation of Islam after the organization disbanded upon the Honorable Elijah Muhammad's physical transition to the Ancestral Realm in 1975. In true professor fashion, my brother provided background information on Minister Farrakhan and shared the powerful mission that he was on and the impact that these teachings were having in his life and the lives of people of African and Indigenous Ancestry throughout America and beyond. Prior to watching the video, I remember intentionally affirming to myself to maintain an open mind, as I was still carrying some resistance to my brother's style of awakening the masses that I held years prior with the Bob Marley lessons.

We all sat in the playroom and watched the video of *The Minister*, which lasted for about three hours! I was amazed by the power of his voice, fluency, courage, and profound love for Black people. I don't remember the topic of his speech, yet I do know that his voice and message deeply penetrated my heart and mind. I remember viewing myself from an elevated and expanded consciousness. I also began to think about my specific role in improving the conditions of my community and my responsibility to contribute to our collective quest for freedom and self-determination. As a family we reflected on what we had observed. My father expressed that he didn't agree with some of the political positions, yet really valued and respected the message centered on morality and righteousness. My mother enjoyed the message of self-determination and was impressed by the wealth of knowledge and the Minister's engaging style of delivery. I was profoundly impacted by the message. I know that my reflection with my family didn't capture all of what I was thinking and feeling as I didn't have the vocabulary to convey the thoughts and emotions that were emerging. As a reflective person by nature, I needed more time to process. I was also intentional about holding back my enthusiasm as I didn't want my brother to mar the integration of the message by overloading me with the meaning of each part of the three-hour lecture. I remember as I began to incorporate the message, I was grateful for the exposure and I revisited the VHS on my own to glean not only the content of the message, but also the Spiritual authority of a man like Minister Farrakhan who embraced and continues to avail himself to be a vessel for his Divine purpose and boldly lives his mission.

As more interest and questions emerged, we decided to attend mosque services and study groups. The first time going to the renowned Mosque #7 in Harlem was unforgettable. I remember as we entered, we were immediately met by members of the Fruit of Islam, the security and disciplinary branch of the Nation of Islam (NOI), who searched us for weapons and any items that were not appropriate for entry into the Mosque. As we were being searched, the brothers communicated their greetings in a welcoming and respectful tone, which countered the discomfort of being examined from head to toe. Once we entered the main venue, we were greeted warmly by more brothers and directed to our seats. It was clear that we were in a very orderly, controlled, and disciplined environment where protocols, standards of operation and a high urgency for safety were top priorities.

As we settled in our seats, one of the Ministers approached the podium. My first impression was how young he looked and how poised and confident he walked as he approached the rostrum. He greeted the congregation with the traditional Islamic greeting words of peace, "*As-Salaam-Alaikum*" (Peace be unto you). The group responded, "*Wa-Alaikum-Salaam*, Sir" (Unto you be peace). As he completed the opening ritual introduction, he began to delve into a preliminary message for the day. I was impressed by someone who looked to be my age and possessed so much knowledge, confidence, conviction, eloquence, and presence. He introduced himself as Brother Jason X. He was extremely sharp in appearance and speech. His youthful energy and ability to convey the teachings was inspiring and it charged me to go deeper in my self-examination and Know Thyself studies. Brother Jason X was the Assistant Minister during this era (late 80s-early

90s) and his 15–20-minute introduction was the warmup for the now departed Minister (in the NOI they now refer to all Ministers as Student Ministers) Kevin X (later to be known as Abdul Hafeez Muhammad). Brother Minister Kevin was also young in his appearance and was powerfully magnetic. His inviting Spirit, captivating voice, deep wisdom, commanding presence, and personable energy left me desiring to learn more about the NOI and challenged me to increase my study, be intentional about my unfolding purpose and continue to cultivate my voice through writing, speaking, and teaching.

Having the Know Thyself ideologies prior to entering Hampton University in 1987, provided a sturdy foundation to pursue higher education with a purpose and create the social parameters that were essential to resist the omnipresent invitations to the adventures of the recreational pleasures of college. I continued to study, learn, and practice Islam as taught by the Honorable Elijah Muhammad. I also attended Jummah services and engaged with Muslims from all denominations. This was a perfect discipline to enter my next stage of learning and maturation. With my thirst to continue to learn about our people's narratives and identify what my contribution would be to our legacy, I continued to explore African-centered philosophies and practices while simultaneously studying the Islamic faith. In addition to raising my expectations in all my life pursuits, the quest for self-knowledge also helped me to divert my energy from the daily temptations that college life presented. I'm talking about sex, drugs, 40 ounces, partying, and all other appeals to lower chakra living.

I created the narrative that Islam and African-centered Righteousness would be my protective shield from the culture of "slackness." I created my own agreements that when I stepped out in African attire or suits and bow ties that I was shielded, and my image would protect me from engaging in any perverse thoughts or behaviors. In my times of weakness or when temptation got the best of me, I was sure not to carry the thoughts or imagery of African-centeredness or Islamic representation, which I associated with righteousness and Superpowers, into the reckless "kryptonite" activities. I recall a time in my first year at Hampton, as I was still gradually integrating my new identity, my friend and I were drinking a 40 of Old English 800, also known as "Old Gold." As we progressively entered an altered sloppy state of unconsciousness, he asked me a question about my thoughts regarding the views of Elijah Muhammad that were expressed in his book, *Message to the Black Man in America.* I curtly responded to his question by saying, "We're not gonna disrespect these teachings by discussing them in the state of mind that we're in." Not only would it have completely disrupted the disoriented state that I chose to enter, it would have also violated what I now considered to be sacred teachings. In my mind, these discussions should never occupy the same space at the same time. I made sure that they never did as I was quickly bringing closure to a life that didn't align with the knowledge, beliefs, values, and practices that I was accepting.

Now in separate environments (I at Hampton University and Rod at the University of South Carolina), my brother and I were experiencing a higher calling, rituals, trials, enlightenments, and celebrations that were culturally centered and gateways to guiding us to missions that influenced the men that we were becoming and the values that served as pillars in our lives. Through African and Indigenous schools of thought, my brother and I continued to raise our awareness, cross thresholds, and incorporate sacred virtues and practices into our daily lives as we navigated our young adulthood and influenced the communities that we chose to serve.

The Sankofa (retrieving of the past while creating the future) Reflections of my life journey through the mirrors and lenses of my formal and informal initiations and passages serve as a guide for this book. Unlike Indigenous African and Aboriginal people, our passages in the Western world were not formalized and deeply rooted in the uninterrupted traditions, rituals, values, and norms that were maintained without disturbances from European captors and external foreign influences. *Crossing the Threshold; Embracing the Call: Conceptualizing, Co-Creating and Building Community Through Rites of Passage* will help to guide a new generation of Rites of Passage facilitators through the timeless pillars, concepts, and frameworks that support contextualizing the transformational initiation experiences that have occurred in their personal lives. It will provide the tools for designing passages for future generations, thereby restoring a sacred and timeless method for optimal levels of community building, which is the foundation for the harvesting of affirmative identity, sacred gifts and the actualization of one's Divine purpose.

Crossing the Threshold is a representation of a lifelong journey of my passages, coupled with 30 years of professional experiences of conceptualizing, designing, implementing, co-creating, and facilitating rites of passages in every community that I have been blessed to serve.

(Left) Rodney Anthony Patterson and Mark Elliot Patterson Bronx, NY, 1974

(Left) Dr. RA Ptahsen Shabazz and Kamau Ptah.
Greenburgh, NY, 2014

CHAPTER ONE

THE CALL

"The purpose of life is a life with a purpose."

Immortal Technique

Call: 1: A strong inner impulse toward a particular course of action especially when accompanied by conviction of divine influence. 2: The vocation or profession in which one customarily engages.

Framing the Call

The Call conveys the highest ideals of what a rite of passage represents. It is the manhood vision, mission and challenge that will begin the process of initiation/learning. "The call" defines the big picture ideals for the manhood journey. They are essential questions, core concepts, lexicon, applied skills, formal assessment, informal assessment, character expectations and unconventional tests/trials. The distinct difference in a formal rites of passage call is it involves the entire community, and it is ritualized and ceremonial. The intent is to be aspirational, inspirational and leave an indelible imprint in the hearts and minds of all who are present for The Call.

Key Components When Making The Call

- 🕊 Articulate the vision, mission, and rationale for an initiation rite, particularly in the 21st Century. Explain what the assignment will be for our time together.

- 🕊 Convey to the boys, young men, their families, and communities that by accepting this you are invested in identifying, claiming, and living from the most authentic expression of your gifts and developing purpose.

- 🕊 Examine the question, "Why rites of passage for boys and young men of African, Indigenous and Latinx Ancestry?"

- 🕊 Inform the community about the expectations of this initiation and their role in helping to support the young men during the rites process.

- 🕊 Describe who our boys and young men will be upon completing the rite of passage experience, What knowledge, skills and values will they possess? How will our community be stronger after their initiation?

The Champion Call

My first significant call did not take on the formalities of a structured and designed invitation. I was thrust deep into an experience that I did not have the opportunity to choose. Once you sign up for life, your calls are presented in overt, subtle, and sometimes unexpected ways. My first call, after my birth, was to the athletic initiation of track and field. Prior to my first meet, I recall running carefree and feeling a sense of power through speed. My older brother and I would race anytime we had a family outing. I recall my father, always teaching us the proper running arm technique and encouraging us to practice our form. When my father observed us running, there was always a spark in his eyes that registered as pride. My father ran track in high school and developed a deep passion and love for the discipline. Though he never fully reached his maximum potential as a runner due to injuries, he learned a great deal about the art and science of track and field. He introduced me and my brother to the sport when I was five years old.

After finishing my first season as a track athlete, the choice was up to me to respond to The Calls after every season. To be competitive, the sport demands you to go through the rigorous training regiment, which requires enduring pain and confronting your fears. Each season I had to make the choice to challenge my mind, body, and spirit to push beyond the thresholds that would take me to prominent levels of performance. The trials of training involved cramps, charley horses (muscle spasms), vomiting, nausea, headaches, shin splints, extreme soreness and at times pulled muscles. The glory of being a respected runner involved persisting through practices that you knew would be painful and discomforting.

The sport also demanded aspirants to develop the will and mindset that would push you beyond your fears. Every week you confronted the nervous energy of performing at your maximum level. The pre-race rituals and self-talk were necessary to challenge the "butterflies" that would surface from the time that the announcer would call your event. I would learn how to summon the warrior within to confidently show up to the starting line to compete against some of the top runners in my age category and attempt to achieve personal best times.

For fourteen seasons of my life, I responded to the track and field call and learned indelible and transferable lessons through the arduous yet rewarding competitive process. The discipline of the sport continues to show up for me as I have learned to approach life with the intention to perform at my maximum level in all my endeavors and apply a focused mindset and willpower to be fully present to the metaphoric races of my life.

As your eyes are absorbing these words, know that your Spirit called and guided you to this book, which serves as an initiation or a rite of passage that reconnects you to your true self. This call is summoned to activate the dormant Spiritual intelligences and qualities that guide you to the threshold of your Divine purpose. The Akoben (War Horn) has sounded for us to remember the reason for our being, the unfolding of our sacred missions, the assignment that we are here to fulfill. This process is similar for us all. We made an agreement for Spirit to occupy a body to learn and teach valuable lessons. These lessons or trials are initiations for us to realize the meaning of our existence. The journey that we have chosen to pursue necessitates that we forget our Divine assignment upon our birth and experience life ordeals as a curriculum guide to reconnect the fragmented pieces of our memory. Malidoma Somé, a West African healer, medicine man, scholar and Indigenous Spiritual Technologist stated that "the process of being born tends to erase our memory of why we came here." With each trial, there is a recognition of the true and authentic self that is reborn, as we shed the conditioned self (the aspect of our identity and image that we feel protects us and helps us survive in the physical world).

Whether you grew up in a culture that was cognizant of the process of "becoming" and intentionally designed initiation rites or were in an environment that was disconnected from these Indigenous practices, the path to self-actualization follows the same universal elements and phases, (which will be explained in the chapter on the phases of a rite of passage). Somé emphasizes, "Whether they are raised in an Indigenous culture or modern culture, there are two things that people crave; the full realization of their innate gifts, and to have these gifts approved, acknowledged and confirmed." He goes on to further validate the informal, unintentional, and unplanned experiences that occur in the West to be as significant and present as similar ordeals that exist in Indigenous African rites; he asserts:

> *"It is to point out that these westerners may underestimate the depth of their own learning and life experiences. Many people would agree that living in the west has its own dangers, which are like the dangers to which African youth are exposed during the rituals of initiation.*
>
> *Westerners meet with tragedy, with powers beyond their control and with challenges that present opportunities for growth*

and transformation. These challenges must be recognized as ini-
tiatory, even though this initiation is disorganized, unpredict-
able, and informal, unlike the carefully orchestrated initiatory
challenges presented to Indigenous people. Westerners, like their
indigenous counterparts, experience initiation in some form and
in a constant manner throughout their life. A person who gets
fired at the job faces a life-transforming challenge that must be
considered initiatory. A couple facing crisis in their relationships,
such as separation or divorce, is on an initiatory path. Initiation
is simply a set of challenges presented to an individual so that he
or she may grow. Consequently, the troubles we encounter in our
paths in the modern world are initiatory to the extent that each
one of them is life changing."

Consistent with the Indigenous meaning of initiation, Yaya Diallo (African Drummer, Healer, and Cultural Custodian from the Fula and Minianka ethnic groups of Mali) asserts, "Initiations were created in our culture expressly to help people realize new strengths within themselves by surmounting difficulties and voluntarily enduring suffering. Initiations are designed to enlarge the initiates' vision of the world. In Minianka, the word initiation implies to die. Through the trials of the initiation old routines are broken, and the initiate moves on the next stage." (Diallo and Hall p. 64)

The initial step to the process of becoming is answering The Call and accepting the Divine assignment of what you are here to teach and to learn. According to Chike Akua, renowned author, cultural custodian, master educator and scholar in *Honoring Our Ancestral Obligations: 7 Steps to Black Student Success*:

"A calling is your purpose for being on the planet; it is your rea-
son for being. Traditional African spirituality (and many other
religious, cultural, and spiritual traditions) tells us that all of us
have been sent here for a powerful and particular purpose. Tradi-
tional African systems of education (rites of passage, initiations,

transformational disciplines) were aimed at helping one under-
stand the nature of their calling and then equipping them with
skills to execute and live their calling with character, conscious-
ness, and commitment."

In Indigenous cultures throughout the world, there is nothing that exists that does not have a purpose. All animated life has a specific function to fulfill that contributes to the greater good of the Universe. One's purpose or Divine calling is the predominant drive that subconsciously and consciously governs human existence. The greatest meaning of human existence is to identify, claim and live a purpose (Higher Calling). In Somé's ethnic group, the Dagara people "believe that everyone is born with a purpose, and that this purpose must be known to ensure an integrated way of living. People ignorant of their purpose are like ships adrift in a hostile sea. They are circling around." Akua confirms this notion when he suggests, "If you don't know your purpose, others will assign you a purpose. So, if they don't know their purpose, society assigns young Black males the purpose of making money for them as inmates doing slave labor." (Akua', *Honoring Our Ancestral Obligations: 7 Steps to Black Student Success*)

Before we proceed any further, it is significant for me to state my calling and Divine purpose and establish a context for all of those who are interested in learning the rites of passage framework to support the boy to man journey.

My purpose is to be a vehicle for the ancient Indigenous Spiritual technologies, sacred wisdom teachings and healing modalities that our Ancestors practiced for the optimal health (Spiritual, mental, emotional, and physical) of our families, communities, nations, and civilizations. I am here to help restore these ancient Spiritual modalities and the transformational disciplines that facilitate the remembrance of our Divine purpose, mission and calling. One of the primary mechanisms that I have embraced as the tool for the retrieval of one's purpose is the initiatory rite of passage process. My assignment is to restore our sacred identity and help us to heal from the Spiritual, mental, and emotional trauma of enslavement, colonization, and centuries of oppression.

For thirty years I have married the ancient rite of passage process to Western conventional educational systems that have helped guide thousands of boys and young men of Indigenous Ancestry to the threshold of their developing purpose. I have gleaned wisdom from Indigenous archetypes, symbols, wisdom teachings and transformational disciplines to address the identity crisis that has plagued our communities for centuries. Whether in my role as a teacher, program director, or consultant, I have approached my practice as a custodian of the wisdom traditions and methods of those who created sophisticated systems of educating and socializing children to "Know Thyself." *In Crossing the Threshold; Embracing the Call: Conceptualizing, Co-Creating and Building Community Through Rites of Passage,* I will share the core components and phases of the rite of passage process that integrates these Indigenous frameworks to facilitate the transition from boyhood to manhood in a modern-day context. The charge that I have accepted has challenged me to use this ancient modality to address the miseducation and toxic socialization of one of the most vulnerable populations in the Western world, Black and Brown boys. As a descendant of African and Indigenous ancestry, and a member of the African Diaspora, I have infused the best of our traditions and have designed passages to affirm the best of who we are as a people. The approach has been to meet young people where they are and reintroduce them to the concepts, practices, and ideals of their Ancestors to awaken their ancestral blood memory, which stores the keys to their personal powers.

Crossing the Threshold offers a framework for people who are interested in creating a rites of passage experience for boys and young men of Indigenous Ancestry (African, Turtle Islanders, Aboriginal descendants). I will serve as your *Jegna* (cultural custodian) for your process as we journey to the interior of your soul and activate the dormant qualities that carry your blood memory. This passage will provide you with the opportunity to reflect, reset, recalibrate, nd reimagine your your life.

Additionally, it will support you with identifying, claiming, and living your Divine purpose. As in all passages, you will have to experience trials that will earn you the title, responsibilities, and privileges of a rites of passage facilitator. Upon the completion of this initiatory process, you will possess the fundamental knowledge and skills to be able to design and facilitate a rite of passage experience for boys and young men in your families and communities.

Kamau Ptah making The Call to young men at the
Annual Eagle Academy for Young Men Mentoring Summit
Eagle Academy for Young Men, Bronx, NY 2019
Credit for photograph – Matthew Fuego, Mat Media.

The Rites of Passage Call to Families

As a *Jegna* initiate, one of your primary responsibilities will be to engage the families and convey the meaning, purpose, and benefits of the Rites of Passage practice. Here is where you will begin to establish the co-creative process and learn about the boys, young men, and their families. As you prepare to make "The Call" to the families, the following thoughts will help you to consider the role that families will contribute to the Rites of Passage process.

A child's first entry into the world represents his or her first rite of passage. The parents/guardians and family are called immediately to think about who they are as a clan and how they will educate, nurture, and socialize the child. Upon the birth of the child, parents are thrust into a rite of passage that places them directly in the storm of lifelong trials that have them confront the core of their knowledge, belief systems and virtues as they must contemplate and figure out how they will help their child navigate life. The essential charge is to determine how they will support their son to arrive at their mission with the competencies necessary to function as a healthy child and enter adulthood with the skills, intelligences, and principles necessary to operate as a strong adult prepared to contribute to the advancement of family, community, nation, and world.

In most cases, it is the family that responds to the call for their sons to participate and experience the Rites of Passage. After hearing the call and being informed about the practice, many parents are excited to have their sons participate. At this stage of adolescence, however, boys, and young men for the most part will not choose to participate in an experience that is designed to challenge them at their core and support them in their boy to man journey. In fact, many adults would not consciously choose experiences where their vulnerabilities are exposed, and trials are created to take them out of their comfort zones.

The parent role in the rites of passage process is extremely significant as they will be charged with 1) reinforcing the virtues and practices learned, 2) supporting the preparation of the boys and young men for their trials and 3) holding their sons accountable to complete the assignments with integrity and a commitment to excellence. The parents provide substantive ideals, values and content that inform the curriculum and instructional focus. To maximize the passage experiences, the primary caretakers and advocates of the boys and young men must be familiar with the philosophy, practices, expectations, and commitments necessary to reinforce the tenets of the passage. Additionally, it would benefit the families to be aware of the mental and emotional discomfort that the boys and young men will be experiencing during their rites journey.

The Rites of Passage call to families also helps parents clarify how to support their boys and young men in identifying, claiming, and living their purpose. The boyhood to manhood journey must be intentional about the tenets, skills and experiences that are essential for the rites of passage process. The decisions that influence the men that our boys will become *must be* contextualized with thoughtful practices and experiences that parents help to design *and plan*.

As *Jegna* aspirants, it will be essential for you to guide the parents/guardians and families through a process that helps you to gain insight to their vision of manhood, core values, family strengths, challenges, traditions, and opportunities to cross thresholds. The following are questions to support the collaborative process centered on actualizing the family's vision of the boy to man rites experience:

- Who is your son? Describe him at this phase of his journey. What are his interests, gifts, talents, aspirations, challenges, fears, and passions?

- What does he need (Spiritually, mentally, emotionally, and physically)?

- Who are you raising him to become?

- What are your belief systems?

- What are some rituals, customs, and traditions that your family practices?

- What knowledge, values and skills do our sons need to thrive in the 21st century? What does manhood mean in the 21st century?

- Who is currently providing socialization experience for our sons? Are you satisfied with the outcomes of this socialization? Explain.

- What are the top concerns about your son at this phase of his life? Why do you have these concerns?

- What formal and informal experiences helped to usher you into adulthood?

- What do you consider to be the essential components of manhood? How do you convey these virtues and practices to your son?

- What do we want him to inherit from our family? What do we need to do to break undesirable patterns of destructive behaviors that exist in our family?

- How are you preparing your son for young manhood? What are you intentionally teaching, guiding him towards and modeling for him?

- What does manhood mean in your family? Who were the adults who were instrumental in your child to adult transition? What did they teach you?

- Create a list of themes, concepts, values, and skills that we would want our son to master by the age of eighteen.

- Upon moving out of our home, your son will know, value and be able to…

- What changes must we make for your son's greatest possibilities to manifest?

- What does healthy manhood look like for our family?

- How do we rear our children amid modern conditions that have been created by historic and persistent conditions of trauma?

- Who are we on the other side of the painful memories and patterns that are present in our family? For my son to reach his maximum potential, I know that I/we must…

Trial for the Families—Letter to Our Son

Once you have facilitated envisioning conversations and experiences with families regarding their son's boy to man journey, you will charge the parents/guardians to write a heart-centered letter to their sons. The following reflects the rationale, framework, and instructions for writing the letter.

As people of African and Indigenous ancestry, we have powerful stories that are testimonies to our heritage of brilliance, pride, and resilience. Resilience is rooted in a tenacity of spirit—a determination to embrace all that makes life worth living even in the face of overwhelming odds. When we have a clear sense of **identity** and **purpose,** we are more resilient because we can hold fast to our vision of a better future. Much of our resilience comes from family and community—from the relationships that allow us to lean on each other for support when we need it.

Our stories are purposeful in helping to inspire us to establish a vision for ourselves and our children, who are deserving of the optimal experiences and conditions that will usher them to the highest standards of excellence and ensure that they contribute to our powerful legacy as a people.

The purpose of a parent, guardian, or fictive kin writing a "Letter to My Son" is for you to reflect on your family's legacy and to articulate the vision, expectations, and values that you desire for your son to exemplify as he transitions from childhood to adulthood.

This sacred document should be visible in his room or placed in a special scrapbook. Your letter should serve as a reminder of who he is with respect to what it means to be a member of your family, culture, and community.

As you prepare your son for the Rites of Passage experience, the following questions will help you to reflect on your vision for his boy to man journey. Answer the questions below as thoroughly as possible and use your responses to create a letter that reflects on what his life means to the family, his gifts, and your vision for what healthy manhood looks like from the perspective of the values and ideals that your family upholds. This affirmative letter will serve as a guide to help ground your son in his identity formation and provide a framework for the daily decisions that he makes during this phase of his life.

Additionally, the letter will be shared during his induction ceremony and will serve as a significant artifact to reflect on during his

Rites of Passage process and other major milestones that occur in his life.

- ❧ Describe your child's birth and what it meant to you and your family.

- ❧ What does your son's name mean? Describe his naming process (how was his name chosen)?

- ❧ What makes your child unique (talents, qualities, etc.)?

- ❧ What are you noticing about his maturing Divine mission/purpose/calling?

- ❧ Describe your son's journey (major accomplishments, challenges, attributes, etc.) from: Birth - 7 years, 8 - 14 years, 15 - present.

- ❧ Who are his people? Where do they come from? What are their belief/knowledge systems? What must he do to honor his family and culture? What do you feel he must let go of to ascend to the next chapter of his life? What do you feel the family must let go of for him to have permission to ascend to the next phase?

- ❧ From your perspective, what does manhood mean? What experiences (educational and social) have been intentional in his boy to man journey?

- ❧ How do you plan to support him through his journey to adulthood? What significant experiences do you feel are essential for his transition into adulthood?

- ❧ What will he know and be able to do upon the completion of his first 21 years of life? What type of man do you desire for your son to become?

The Call to the Boys and Young Men

As a *Jegna* initiate, setting the stage for the boys and young men will be a high priority. How do you make a call to awaken someone out of their comfortable state of "slumber"? How do you inspire boys and young men to embrace the initiation process that calls for their gifts and purposes to be activated along with the responsibilities that come with living their calling? Establishing the rites of passage experience as an adventure to identify, claim and live from their "Superpowers," will appeal to boys and young men as it is an unconscious inclination for pre-adolescent and adolescent boys/young men to take chances, challenge fears, acquire intelligence and skills essential to knowing and mastering themselves. The absence of formalized rites of initiation for boys and young men can lead them to create passages that are informed by immature choices, and trials that are disconnected from life affirming community norms, values and customs that are rooted in legacy. As you prepare to make the call to boys and young men, consider the following thoughts as pillars for establishing the rationale.

Framing the call for boys and young men of African and Indigenous Ancestry is one of the most revolutionary acts of our era. From a pro-active view, the call to the rites of passage is a self-determining act, which charges our communities to craft transformational experiences that support the healthy identity formation of our boys and young men. The context is our socio-cultural identity that centers us in a narrative that speaks to the best of who we are and helps us design experiences that yield our greatest possibilities for the times that we live in. Our Ancestors throughout the African and Indigenous earth created highly sophisticated education and socialization systems that helped usher children into adulthood and prepared them to identity their gifts, powers, intelligences, and Divine purpose. Both boys and girls in these cultures earned the privileges and responsibilities of entering the adult community with a clear understanding of their significant roles in maintaining the collective values, worldview, social order, customs, and ways of knowing and being. Also, they were given the charge to advance the legacy of their families and communities.

The Rites of Passage process is our birthright. Boys and young men who experience the rites of passage initiation with their peer group, create lifelong kinship bonds that foster accountability, brotherhood, and shared experiences of enduring trials, crossing thresholds, and celebrating milestones. These elements define their becoming process from boyhood to manhood. The call to manhood in the modern era will help to build the immunity in a society that is unwavering in its efforts to retard the maturation process for boys and young men of African and Indigenous Ancestry. Though they may experience the dehumanization process dictated by the systems of White Supremacy, our boys and young men will play a significant role in eradicating these destructive systems. Like no other time, our boys and young men will possess a new and powerful potion against any resistance to their self-actualization. The more attempts to suppress their vision, voices, and creativity, the greater and more powerful their Divine expression will emerge as an armor. Their initiation will serve as preparation to create a world that will be governed by truth, justice, harmony, order, balance, reciprocity, propriety, and Love (Ma'at).

For the past five hundred years, there has been a perpetual onslaught on the Spirit, mind, character and bodies of Black and Brown boys and men. The intention and strategy were designed to ensure that Black and Brown boys never achieve full maturation into manhood. In patriarchal Western societies, Black and Brown men present the greatest threat to White male domination and "supremacy." Dr. Nathan and Julia Hare state that "in human societies, elaborate systems have arisen to regulate the male's function. Consequently, in a patriarchal society where men predominate among the rulers, it is the oppressed male that poses the primary threat to the rulers, and it is the oppressed that must be derailed." (Hare 1985. P 16). As the old-world continues to crumble, the opportunity for our boys and young men to have a non-attached relationship with trauma will position them to break the cycle of memories that have weighted our existence. We will rise above our painful memories as winds beneath the wings of our Ancestors greatest visions for our collective lives.

As we have entered a new age, our boys and young men will be handlers of powers that their predecessors never had access to or at least not in the past five hundred years. How will we prepare them to responsibly manage this power? How can we teach them to appreciate and value what our traumas taught us, yet not allow the narrative to cripple them? What will their presence be from now until eternity without the inheritance and influence of the painful memories that have been passed down for centuries? Our modern initiations can reinterpret our trauma and create the necessary healing that is essential for the greatest expression of what it means to be a healthy Spiritual power in the human flesh.

The Call to young men at the 11th Annual Coalition of Schools Educating Boys of Color Gathering of Leaders Young Men's Passage University of Texas, Austin, Texas, 2017

Trial for the Boys and Young Men

The boys, young men and their families that have accepted the call are immediately presented with trials that will help them deeply reflect on their lives, their calling, gifts, fears, pains, and strategies for claiming and living their Divine purpose. The Indigenous notion that we were born to contribute to the evolution of human consciousness and contribute to the planet and the human experience directed by our unique purpose is lost in modern education and socialization systems. The rites of passage process are designed to confront and persevere through fears, pain memories, and achieve a higher meaning for our existence.

Prior to having the boys and young men respond to their questions, *Jegnas* themselves are charged with the assignment to answer the following questions as honestly as possible. Using words, images, symbols, and music to provide descriptions of who you are from your core (the most authentic and true version of yourself), *Jegnas* will use the responses to these questions to create an oath (see definition and prompts below). These questions will put you on the path to making choices that honor the reason you were created and begin to attract the people, resources and experiences that will guide your life passages.

You would not be presented with these questions if you were not ready. Do not be intimidated by the depth of these questions. Let your heart guide the process and do not judge what comes through as your answers. You are now embarking on a *Jegna* journey that will guide you to your destined path to greatness. Your families, communities, nation, and world need your mission, gifts, powers, intelligence, creativity, and presence. We are grateful that you have responded to the call!

As *Jegna* initiates, it is necessary for you to respond to these questions prior to giving the charge to the boys and young men. It will also be a significant trial for you to convey these thought-provoking questions and translate them to the boys and young men that will experience this trial. It may be challenging to craft words for these questions, so consider story boards, collages, songs, archetypes and themes from Avatar, *Black Panther* and other contemporary fables that have rites of passage and Hero's Journey narratives.

Allow Me to Introduce Myself

1. Who am I?

2. Whose am I (Who are my people, what are their values/beliefs/practices)?

3. What is my mission in life?

4. How will I fulfill my mission?

5. What are the challenges that are obstacles in realizing my mission?

6. What habits do I need to change to become the person I am being called to be?

7. What fears am I ready to confront?

8. What painful memories am I ready to let go?

9. Who will my mission serve?

10. What gifts do I have to give to the world?

11. Describe how people experience my gifts and purpose?

12. How will my mission impact my family, community, nation, and world?

13. What will people say about my life work when I become an Ancestor? What will be my legacy?

14. What do I need to do to further empower my life?

Oath Statement and Affirmations:

Now that you have explored some of life's essential questions, use the content to create an Oath Statement. If you are on a quest to actualize (see your vision, come to reality) your life Nia (purpose), it is important to create an oath and affirmations to keep your vision alive. Every decision that you make in life should be guided by the ideals that are represented in your oath. You should always keep your oath nearby to refocus yourself when the chaos of life begins to appear and complicate your path.

The following are some recommended thoughts and terms to support you in creating your pledge.

Oath: A solemn, formal declaration or promise to fulfill a pledge, often calling upon a Divine presence (Higher Power) as a witness.

Affirmation: A statement spoken and accepted as truth.

Assignment: Create an oath that includes your commitment to live by your values and highest aspirations. Additionally, create affirmations to reinforce what your oath is conveying. The affirmations will convince your mind that you are what your oath states. Once you know that you are the words in your oath, you will attract all the resources that are necessary to achieve your life purpose. Review the oath below as an example:

OATH

In honor of _____ I, _____ make a commitment to....

I also devote myself to upholding the attitudes and behaviors of _____

Lastly, I take this oath to fulfill my vision as a _____

Example:

In honor of The Most High, Spirit Guides, Ascended Masters, Sacred Plants, Water, Nature, Air, Earth, Fire, Minerals, and the legacy of my Ancestors, I, Kamau Ptah, make a commitment to availing myself to be a vehicle for the sacred traditions of the Rite of Passage initiation practice and Indigenous Spiritual Healing Technologies. I also devote myself to studying, practicing, and upholding the attitudes and behaviors of the best of what manhood reflects from my Spiritual and Cultural knowledge and beliefs. I will strive to operate with Spiritual integrity, cultural virtues, authenticity, and LOVE! Lastly, I take this oath to fulfill my vision to become the highest expression and vehicle for the Rites of Passage practice, Indigenous Spiritual Healing Technology, Djembe transformational practices, and methods for the elevation of human consciousness.

Affirmations

I am a powerful expression of healing for my people (primarily melanated people).

I am a present and Loving husband, father, and family man.

I am a keeper of the Ancient, Sacred rite of passage practices.

I am a Loving family man, leader, healer, teacher, Spiritual Warrior, and cultural custodian.

I am a bridge from antiquity to the future providing Love, Wisdom, Truth, and Self-Knowledge.

I am a Spiritual and Cultural Abolitionist.

I am a Spiritual Being having a human experience.

The Rites of Passage Facilitators' Call to Action

If you have journeyed the path to manhood in melaninated skin, it is likely that you have endured horrific trials that were designed to sever you completely from the memory of your Indigenous ways of knowing and being. These dehumanizing tactics were used to ensure that boys of African and Indigenous Ancestry would never mature to become self-determined men.

There have always been those who resisted oppression from the inception of European colonization and enslavement. Across all planes of existence (spiritual, mental, emotional, or physical) resides a resolute and determined quest to rekindle the Indigenous understanding of self. This perspective views the African and Indigenous individual as a multifaceted being, simultaneously existing within the limitations of the individual and transcending temporal boundaries. At its core, this notion of self encompasses the soul, the mental faculties, the physical form, the social/emotional intelligences, and ancestral connection, which forms a holistic paradigm of existence that resonates through time and space.

The ones heeding the summons to guide boys and young men through rites of passage embark on a journey of initiation to ascend to the revered status of a *Jegna*. In Amharic (official language of Ethiopia), *Jegna* personifies the essence of bravery, embodying the role of custodian of culture, the rights of the people, and the sacred lands they inhabit. Fear is unfamiliar to the *Jegna*, for they are keepers of unyielding truth, their integrity solid, their essence meshed with the well-being and protection of their kin. They stand ready to lay down their lives for the community they champion. Jenoch, the plural of *Jegna*, are the select few who have navigated the trials of battle, demonstrating unparalleled courage and resilience. They have etched their legacy through unwavering dedication to the protection of their people, their lands, and the cherished heritage they safeguard. Their commitment shines through the excellence of their endeavors, their steadfast dedication serving as a beacon for the advancement and nurturing of the next generation, ensuring the preservation, and thriving of their people, their place, and their culture.

Trial for *Jegna* Aspirants:

Jegnas in training, respond to the following questions and use your responses to create a Declaration Statement that conveys your intentions, capacity, and vision as a facilitator of the sacred rites of passage process. This declaration will be presented to the community during the induction ceremony. Your role as a *Jegna* is a public statement that you have accepted the call to serve as a custodian of the principles and practices of this indigenous transformational discipline and technology.

1. In your journey to manhood, identify the calls that you responded to that represented initiations in your life.
2. Recall what resonated with you about the call.
3. What were the trials during the initiation? How were you tested? What struggles did you overcome?
4. What were the indelible lessons learned?
5. How do these lessons show up for you in your life today?

6. How will these lessons be apparent in your role as a ROP facilitator?

7. What do you feel was essential about your passage that you know that our boys and young men can benefit from today?

8. Based on your life lessons, what will our boys and young men know, value and be able to do upon experiencing your presence, gifts, purpose, and role as a facilitator?

9. At this stage of life, particularly with the conditions that we are now living in, what call are you hearing? What is becoming a primary focus in your life?

10. What is showing up as affirmative qualities that you are grateful that you have mastered?

11. What is showing up as patterns of thoughts and behaviors that no longer serve you?

12. Who do you envision yourself becoming upon completion of this passage?

13. What do you envision for our boys and young men upon completion of their initiation?

Now that you have surfaced some of your thoughts in response to these essential mission affirming and envisioning questions, use your answers as content to complete your Jegna Declaration Statement below:

Jegna Declaration Statement:

I, *Jegna* _____, have accepted the call to serve as a rite of passage facilitator. My intention to serve in this role is to _____. I have a demonstrated history of _____. This experience will help support my mission as _____. Through engaging with me,

the boys will learn _____ Upon
the successful completion of this rites of passage experience, I envision our boys _____
_____
_____.

The Rites of Passage Call to the Community:

Not every member of a community will have the time or interest to serve
as a *Jegna* of the Rites of Passage process. However, there are some fundamental ways that community members can participate and support
the boys and young men's experience. In addition to the *Jegna's* role of
facilitating the process for the boys and their families, other key responsibilities are informing the community about the mission, core values
and ways to support the boys during their Rite of Passage experience.

There are many themes and topics germane to the rites of passage
journey that the *Jegnas* may not have personal experience or awareness
about in their own narratives. Community members can serve as workshop facilitators on a variety of topics that will not only be enlightening
to the boys and young men, but will also help establish relationships
and connections with significant members of the community that the
initiates may not have access to in their daily routines and where the
adult and child's worlds do not connect consistently. The community's
role in sharing firsthand experiences and narratives will build continuity, cohesion and lifelong bonds with members who sometimes navigate
our neighborhoods anonymously. When community members share
their gifts, purpose and lessons learned in their processes of "becoming," their sense of mission, value and belonging expands and the boys
and young men open to worlds of ideas, thoughts, wonderings, and
possibilities that they never knew existed. The following are some of the
ways that community members can support the rites of passage process:

➤ Sharing their narratives in a Community Building Brotherhood
   Cypher (sacred circle where wisdom, knowledge, reasoning, and
   decisions are collectively shared and processed)

- Creating career shadowing opportunities for the boys and young men

- Establishing apprenticeships and job opportunities for the eligible young men

- Volunteering to chaperone field trips (Make sure all volunteers go through proper screening to be eligible to work with children)

- Participating in the trials, milestone events and celebrations that occur during the Rites of Passage initiation.

- Providing resources (equipment, supplies, funds, food, beverages, etc.)

- Participating in fundraisers.

- Sharing knowledge and resources that reflect the expertise of the adult community members.

- Creating opportunities for the boys and young men to volunteer at events that represent the adult's sphere of influence and obligation.

At the bare minimum, if community members cannot actively be involved in sessions, they can offer affirmative words, compliment the boys and young men on achievements or upstanding behaviors, smile and greet the young men when they see them in the community and always look for an opportunity to acknowledge, affirm, celebrate, and challenge the boys and young men to be the best version of themselves. These simple acts of recognition help to humanize our boys and young men and provide a counter narrative to how society sometimes directs their fear, hate, shame, and low expectations on our boys while never offering them opportunities to express who they truly are. When there is an affirmative assumption about who the boys and young men are, it increases the opportunity for a healthy self-fulfilling prophecy that communicates to the boys and young men that someone sees and acknowledges their Divinity and that they have a safe space to allow their light to shine.

As the *Jegna* Aspirants and initiates participate publicly in their rites of passage experiences, you will be amazed at the response of the community. When men are present and engaging boys in a healthy fashion, it not only intrigues the community, it provides an opportunity for the community members to share in the experience by informally participating. Participation can be as active as someone joining the activity that they are observing or as simple as cheering from the sidelines with encouraging words and gestures of support. No matter how overt or subtle, when the community observes a rites of passage process in real time it activates the Indigenous community persona that generates the thoughts and emotions of belonging. Once the tenets and foundation of community are established, anything is possible.

Pre-Induction Events and Activities:

Up to this point, we have been participating in the preliminary phases of the rites work prior to the induction ceremony. These pre-trials have been helping to lay the groundwork necessary for the formal presentation of the boys, young men and all the participants that will be responsible for the initiates' passage experiences.

In addition to the trials, the Lead *Jegna* and *Jegna* Aspirants must create an opportunity for all participants called to the initiation to gather and establish collective intentions, kinship building opportunities, and exercises that help establish the core values and practices for the initiatory experience. Though you might live and engage as neighbors or colleagues in an organization or institution, that does not translate to operating with clear community commitments. One of the first steps to officially beginning the rites of passage initiation, is to facilitate an Intergenerational gathering to establish the core pillars to the manhood development process. This gathering will help clarify what manhood looks like in your respective communities and will provide the blueprint for the rites of passage journey. The following are recommended questions to facilitate the discussion.

INTERGENERATIONAL COMMUNITY GATHERING

Questions to Consider When Establishing a Rites of Passage Initiative:

- How does our community define manhood?
- What are our community's core values?
- What new lexicon should we be intentional about introducing to establish the ambience and conditions desired by our community?
- What community-wide rituals do we currently have that affirm our boys and young men? How can we build on these rituals?
- Who are the boys and young men in our community? What are their interests, talents, values, aspirations, challenges, fears, and passions?
- What knowledge, values and skills do our boys and young men need for them to thrive in our community and beyond?
- How do we challenge our boys and young men to perform at optimal levels of success: personally, culturally, and academically?
- How do we celebrate the achievements of boys and young men in our community?
- What opportunities are available for our boys and young men to assume leadership roles within our community?
- What trials can we create that would prepare them to take on responsibilities and earn privileges in our community?
- What community resources do we have available to support the holistic education and socialization of our boys and young men?
- How must adults operate to ensure a healthy passage for boys and young men in our community?
- How can the adults be held to a greater level of accountability, model upstanding character and serve as positive role models for our boys and young men?

After discussing these questions, begin to identify the pillars and key components for designing the rites of passage experience that captures the pulse of the community's needs and the outcomes we anticipate upon the successful passage of our boys, young men, and the highest aspirations of our community. The table below is an example of how to format the questions and your answers. You can write the answers in this book but we suggest you consider writing your answers in a journal, notebook or create a file on your computer. Your knowledge will be evolving and you'll want to update your entries.

QUESTIONS	PILLARS AND KEY COMPONENTS FOR DESIGNING THE RITES OF PASSAGE
How does our community define manhood?	
What are our community's core values?	
What new lexicon should we be intentional about introducing to establish the ambience and conditions desired by our community?	
What community-wide rituals do we currently have that affirm our boys and young men? How can we build on these rituals?	

Who are the boys and young men in our community? What are their interests, talents, values, aspirations, challenges, fears, and passions?	
What knowledge, values and skills do our boys and young men need for them to thrive in our community and beyond?	
How do we challenge our boys and young men to perform at optimal levels of success: personally, culturally, and academically?	
How do we celebrate the achievements of boys and young men in our community?	
What opportunities are available for our boys and young men to assume leadership roles within our community?	
What trials can we create that would prepare them to take on responsibilities and earn privileges in our community?	

What community resources do we have available to support the holistic education and socialization of our boys and young men?	
How must adults operate to ensure a healthy passage for boys and young men in our community?	
How can the adults be held to a greater level of accountability, model upstanding character, and serve as positive role models for our boys and young men?	

Rites of Passage *Jegna* Aspirants Training (Facilitators Passage):

The *Jegna* Aspirants initiation will guide the men to the threshold of their identity as *Jegnas*. The initiates will be trained in the art and science of the sacred methods of initiation and transformational discipline techniques. Ideally, the *Jegna* initiation should occur over a period of a year or at a minimum seven months. Once the *Jegna* Aspirant begins to internalize the fundamentals of initiation, he will be able to view life from a rites of passage lens and realize that each trial that he experiences can be regarded as an initiatory experience that brings him closer to actualizing the Divine design and purpose of his life as a *Jegna* Facilitator.

The following are the themes and concepts for the *Jegna* Aspirants Initiation Journey:

- Why Rites of Passage in the 21ˢᵗ century? History, Theory and Practice
- The Journey and Role of the *Jegna*
- The Significant Passages in the Human Experience
- From Maleness to Manhood
- Who Are Our Boys and Young Men?
- The Six Phases of the Rites of Passage
- The Call—Theory and Practice
- Rituals and Indigenous Spiritual Technologies for Building the Internal and External Community
- The Trials—Theory and Practice
- Trauma and Isolation- Entry to Initiation
- Liminality and Vulnerability—The Gateways to Becoming
- Enlightenment—The Great 'Aha' Moments
- Celebration—Theory and Practice
- The Art, Science, Roles, and Responsibilities of *Jegna* Facilitators and Facilitation
- Establishing the Pillars of Manhood from Antiquity to the 21ˢᵗ Century
- The Oath Statement—*Jegna* Aspirants Declaration of Purpose
- *Jegna* Aspirant Trials
- The Ceremonies—Theory and Practice
- Re-Incorporation—Theory and Practice
- Rites of Passage The Legacy of Manhood Development from Antiquity, the Now and Until Eternity
- *Jegna* Rising Ceremony

Pre-Experiences for the Boys and Young Men

As families have determined or are considering their sons' participation in the rites of passage journey, it would be beneficial to observe and engage the boys and young men prior to the induction ceremony. The pre-experiences will help the facilitators learn about the strengths, gifts, powers, and potential of the initiates. Additionally, the boys and young men have an opportunity to connect and build a healthy rapport with the *Jegna* Aspirants. The pre-experiences will help to accelerate the trust that will be necessary during the rites of passage process.

Interacting with the initiates prior to their experience will allow the *Jegna* Aspirants to begin to customize learning strategies and trials that will affirm the initiates' gifts, learning styles and design activities that are centered on their authentic interests and passions. Again, the rites of passage experiences are not something that most boys and young men would choose for themselves. It is extremely important to know as much about them as possible before challenging their character and putting them in formal experiences that expose their vulnerabilities. With the intention of building affirmative relationships, the initiates will be more trusting and willing to explore the unknown aspects of their identity when they know that the adults guiding their experiences have their best interest at heart.

The following are pre-activities that would support the rites of passage process for the boys, young men, and *Jegna* Aspirants:

- Community Building Brotherhood Cypher
- Young Men Centered Panel Discussions (During the *Jegna* Aspirants' Facilitation Training)
- Shadow an initiate during their school day
- Attend a game, concert, faith-based experience, or activity that the Initiate is enthusiastic about and participates in regularly.
- Organize a kick ball, basketball, touch football, video, or board games with the initiates.
- Attend a movie, play, or concert with the initiates
- Participate in a volunteer service activity.

Pre-Experiences for the Parents

The best way to get to know the families and their core values would be to have them reflect on their journey to parenthood and identify the significant passages in their lives. This process will support them in identifying their core values and the daily decisions that they make as parents. There are myriad essential questions. What legacy would I like my child to inherit? What do we value as a family? What rituals, traditions and daily practices help us take daily steps to building our legacy? What cycles in our family patterns are we intentional about breaking? What does manhood look like in our family? What vision do we have for our son when he reaches the age of twenty-one? What metaphoric deaths must happen in our family for our son to actualize the vision we have for him?

The following are some pre-activities that the parents can participate in with the *Jegna* Aspirants to support their son's rite of passage experience:

- Vision Board that reflects the family's values and vision of their son's manhood process.

- Attend a family outing.

- Participate in a workshop and discussion centered on family rituals.

- Attend a cultural event together.

- Establish a book club that focuses on raising Spiritually centered and culturally competent children.

- Design a family game event.

- Attend a sip and paint event centered on a theme that aligns with family and community.

- Participate in a session that identifies and/or establishes the daily rituals and routines that must occur in the household that support the family's vision.

- Participate in a "Letting go" Ceremony that focuses on releasing generational curses, Post and Persistent Stress Disorder

(PPSD) and undesirable family patterns. Also, the ceremony will invite families to affirm their healthy identity and norms that will build their powerful legacy.

Induction Ceremony

Now that the *Jegna* Aspirants have successfully completed their training and the parents and initiates have had some community building activities, we are ready to facilitate the Induction Ceremony. The purpose of this observance is to formally launch the rites of passage and introduce the *Jegnas*, families and initiates to the community. The community is informed of the vision, mission, the rites of passage process and expectations. Once the declarations are made, the elders and community affirm and approve if the initiation will commence.

The following is a template and guidelines for the Induction Ceremony:

Processional—Walk of Integrity

A procession is an organized body of people walking in a formal or ceremonial manner. In many Indigenous cultures, a sacred event is often launched with a processional walk. The entry into the ceremonial space is accompanied by drumming, dancing, or other forms of traditional music. For the Walk of Integrity, I recommend that traditional African, African Diaspora or Indigenous drums open the ceremony.

Drums are the spiritual voice that articulates the collective identity of the people that they represent. This collective voice consists of every member of the living community, the earth, and the Ancestors. The drum call informs the community to gather and be present for the event that is about to take place. The drummers will make the call and lead the procession into the venue where the ceremony will occur. The drumming and dancing help to establish the intention and ambiance for the entire ceremony.

Prior to the young men entering the space, the *Jegna* Aspirants will begin to help the young men establish the right mindset for the ceremony. The energy that the *Jegna* Aspirants create should resemble the experience that an athlete would have before stepping on the field or the court. The intention is to cultivate the Warrior Spirit and prepare the initiates to demonstrate impeccable focus. The *Jegna* Aspirants should lead the young men in affirmative call and response mantras. The following are examples of mantras that I created for the school that I co-founded, the Urban Assembly Academy of History and Citizenship for Young Men (UAAHC):

Call: "What time is it?"

Response: "UAAHC Time!" (Recite two times)

Call: "Brothers are we ready?"

Response: "UAAHC Ready!" (Recite two times)

Call: "Who are we?"

Response: "Men of the past, living in the present, moving towards the future." (Recite two times)

Call: "What hood we rep?"

Response: "Manhood!" (Recite 2 times)?

Call: "What hood we rep?"

Response: "Brotherhood" (Recite 2 times)

Call: "I want for my brother…"

Response: "What I want for myself" (Recite 2 times)

Call: "Retrieve the past"

Response: "Create the future" (Recite 2 times)

Call: "Sharpen your eyes.
          Tune your ears.

So, you know what you see.
Understand what you hear."

Response: "Minute by minute
Hour by hour
As we know Our Story
We know Our POWER!!!

Everyone : UAAHC!!!!!

THE FOLLOWING SHOULD BE EXPLAINED TO THE INITIATES

"Throughout the journey of people of African and Indigenous Ancestry, there have been many pathways that reflect the struggles and victories of our Ancestors' quest for dignity, equality, and justice. The life path of our Ancestors, who have made significant contributions to our people's narrative, can be represented in the notion of footprints. Footprints are the imprints left by a foot or a shoe on the ground or a surface. What imprints of our people's legacy do you represent? Whose footprints are you following? Where are they leading you? What path are your footsteps ordered to walk on? Are your footsteps leading you to the destination you are striving to reach?"

"Today you will participate in a ceremonial processional known as the Walk of Integrity. To have integrity means to have honor and strong moral principles. This Grand Procession of your family, elders, *Jegnas*, *Jegna* Aspirants, school and community leaders and distinguished guests will set the stage for you taking another affirmative step towards healthy boyhood and young manhood. The 'Walk of Integrity' will be a symbolic declaration and commitment to excellence in all areas of your life (mental, emotional, physical, and Spiritual). This walk will signify the mission to do all that is in your power to honor the Creator, your Ancestors, your developing missions, your goals, the best of your family's expectations, and the commitment to your rites of passage process."

Entering the Pathway to Walk with Integrity

Prior to lining up for the Walk of Integrity, the boys and young men will respond to questions centered on expectations and willingness to engage in the rites experience. The facilitators and men from the community will be positioned at stations and the boys will respond to the following questions:

Welcome:

The Rites of Passage is a call to your true and best self. Many boys and young men wear masks to hide their gifts, talents, powers, and wounds. These _____months will give you the opportunity to experience the REAL you. You will be SAFE! Are you willing to continue?

The initiate will proceed to the next facilitator.

Welcome:

During this passage you will be confronted with experiences that have generated fear or caused you some form of discomfort. If or when these memories surface, we encourage you to struggle and embrace the challenges. You will be SAFE! Are you willing to continue?

The initiate will proceed to the next facilitator.

Welcome:

During your Rites of Passage, it is important to have an intention and explore your "Whys" for being here. Why did you come? Why did you respond to this call? What are you seeking during this journey to your true self?

The initiate will respond to the questions.

The lead *Jegna* will state, "At this moment, reflect on what it means to walk with integrity. Remember your Ancestors footprints, marches, and journeys which have influenced who you are and whose you are. Today, you are being called to restore and carry on the legacy of excellence."

As the young men are preparing for the walk, have them reflect on the following questions

(This can be facilitated as a writing exercise or a small group activity):

1. Who are you walking for today?
2. What principles/ideals/virtues will your walk represent?
3. Whose footprints or life path do you follow?
4. What difference will your life walk make in the lives of your family, community, nation, and world?
5. For you to reach your goals in life, what are some of the obstacles (thoughts and behaviors) that you must let go of to be successful?
6. Where will your footprints lead people? What will your footprints remind people of when they study and reflect on your life?

Once the young men have been charged to reflect integrity in their walk, the *Jegnas*, *Jegna* Aspirants and men of the community will blindfold them and upon the sound of the drum call, they will embark on their steps toward the official initiatory journey to manhood.

As the procession concludes, the next significant protocol is seeking an elder's consent to officially begin the ceremony.

Welcome: Opening Remarks

The lead *Jegna* will welcome the participants with a brief statement on the vision for the ceremony. Prior to any other remarks, the *Jegna* will seek permission from the elders to begin the celebration. The following is an example of the protocol:

Permission from Elders:

In traditional African and Indigenous communities throughout the world, elders are viewed as Sacred. The elders are those who have experienced many passages and have accumulated profound wisdom. They are not merely respected for their chronological age; they are revered for their successful passages that they have experienced, and the wisdom earned through mastering life's trials. These elders are the embodiment of what healthy adulthood looks like and they are living examples of the virtues that the boys, young men, and *Jegna* Aspirants are striving to manifest.

The welcoming remarks will be followed by identifying the elders (identified prior to the ceremony and considered as distinguished participants). The lead *Jegna* will establish the rationale for the ceremony and contextualize the significance and intentions for the gathering.

THE FOLLOWING IS AN EXAMPLE OF THE ELDER'S CONSENT PROTOCOL

Introduce the elders and have them stand in front of the venue (have a special table designated for them to sit). If they are not able to stand, they will remain seated. The lead *Jegna* will state the following prompts:

> To our esteemed elders, we seek your permission for the next_____ months to guide our boys and young men to the ways of manhood that has been represented by the best of our sacred traditions and practices.
>
> Do we have your consent?
>
> To our esteemed elders, we seek your permission to facilitate this initiation to guide our boys and young men to the threshold of their identity and purpose.
>
> Do we have your consent?
>
> To our esteemed elders, we ask your permission to lead this ancient process that will cultivate the brilliance in our boys

and young men. We seek to help them activate an insatiable appetite for learning, the desire and courage to lead and the humility to serve.

Do we have your consent?

Lastly, to our beloved elders! We ask you in this critical hour to use the power of your wisdom and influence to encourage all the members of our Village to be present with our boys and young men throughout the entire initiation and to share their knowledge, resources, and experiences with the *Jegnas, Jegna* Aspirants and the initiates as we collectively create a web of support for our boys and young men.

Can you assist us with ensuring that our village helps our young men complete their process by being present (mentally, physically, emotionally, and spiritually)?

Esteemed elder are there any words of wisdom that you can offer to provide guidance, encouragement, and direction to the initiatory process that we are about to embark on?

Thank you elders for your blessings and support!

Libation:

Once the Elder's grant permission for the ceremony to commence, we are now prepared for the Libation Ritual. In African and Indigenous cultures throughout the world, there is an awareness that the Ancestors (deceased members of one's family, blood lineage, and those who share the same genetic makeup) are a significant part of the community. The Ancestors are invited to participate in all the affairs that make up the human experience, particularly ceremonial events.

According to the African and Indigenous view, the Ancestor's role in the lives of the living is to:

- Support optimal health, prosperity and rootedness in place and culture.
- Guide, uplift, and protect their ascendants.

- Invest in outcomes that are beneficial to the family and community.

- Serve as allies for living family members who seek to transform and end difficult intergenerational burdens.

- Provide blessings to major passages in life.

- Contribute to the vitality and healthy balance of life.

- Promote and preserve moral living and the continuation of life upholding virtues.

- Support the building and maintenance of powerful legacies.

- Provide information and messaging that serve as medicine and methods for the wellness of family and community (Foor, pg. 29)

Libation is a ritual of heritage, an offering to honor and please the powers that represent that which is sacred, good, grand, and beyond. It also recognizes the Ancestral lineages and the ecology. Many Indigenous people throughout the world practice this ritual. When facilitating the Libation ritual, we are:

- Summoning the Divine and Ancestors who embody our collective ideals.

- Paying homage to our Ancestors

- Making an offering to the Ancestors

- Celebrating our individual and collective identity

- Requesting a deeper connection and guidance to support each other as family.

- Engaging in a co-creative process where Ancestors assist the living by providing guidance, inspiration, and direction from their elevated view.

- Communicating with our past and our highest ideals

- Making a declaration to identify, claim and live our legacy.

The following are the essential elements necessary for facilitating Libations:

- Have a clear intention aligned with the objectives for the ritual.
- Communicate sincerely as if you are speaking directly to the Ancestors (like they are physically present).
- Create a sacred space (prior to the event burn sage, palo santo, frankincense or copal).
- Convey the aspirations and concerns of the community.
- Play music (If possible, play live acoustic music that creates an ambience for family and community intimacy).
- Powerful closing that offers gratitude for the Ancestors' presence and affirmations that assert that all the outcomes anticipated will be achieved (It is important to transition from an ethereal and aspirational space to a practical plan of action drawing from the inspiration of the ritual).

Sample Libation Protocol:

The Libation Ritual described below is a fundamental method for invoking the presence of the Ancestors. In traditions throughout African and Indigenous America, you will be able to find nuanced and specific ways that ethnic groups summon the Ancestors. These ethnic groups' language, cosmology, folklore, traditions, and their relationship with the land are all significant to the ritual design and expression.

Prior to facilitating the ritual, you will need water and a plant or soil. If your ceremony is outside, you will not need the plant.

The following is one example of how to facilitate the Libation Ritual. It is important to customize the ritual to align with the intentions and objectives that you are planning for your ceremony.

The Lead *Jegna* will facilitate or request an elder, priest, Reverend, Minister, Imam, Spiritual practitioner, etc.

Ritual Facilitator: "Infinite Spirit, we are grateful for your presence in this sacred moment. Thank you for ensuring that our tribute to the Ancestors is performed with the highest expression of Love and is executed with deep sincerity."

Village: "*Ashe*" (Let it be so, and so it is)

Ritual Facilitator: "Great Ancestors, we welcome you into our ceremony today with boundless joy! Thank you for joining us as we prepare to usher our boys to young manhood."

Ritual Facilitator: Pours water.

Village: "*Ashe*"

Ritual Facilitator: Welcome caring loving, compassionate and wise recent Ancestors (deceased from the present to two hundred years ago) in our bloodline. We are grateful that you are present today. We call you and seek your guidance with helping to usher our boys to shining examples of young manhood.

"We now call your names _____"
(participants call the names of their recent personal bloodline Ancestors)

Ritual Facilitator: Pours Water

Village: "*Ashe*"

Ritual Facilitator: "Welcome Indigenous Ancestors. The foundation and genesis of our bloodlines. We are grateful that you are present today. Ancient, wise, compassionate, Loving, and brilliant Ancestors; we call your names to provide us with wisdom, guidance, and direction with guiding our boys to shining examples of young manhood.

We now call the names of our ethnic groups, Indigenous homelands, and bloodline Ancestors from antiquity."

Ritual Facilitator: Pours Water

Village: *"Ashe"*

Ritual Leader: "Welcome Community and Notable Ancestors who made it your mission to advance freedom and the greatest possibilities for people of African and Indigenous heritage. We are grateful for your presence today.

Powerful leaders, teachers, and guides; we now call on your brilliance, courage, visions, and missions with guiding our boys to shining examples of young manhood."

Ritual Facilitator: Pours water.

Village Responds: *"Ashe'"*

Ritual Facilitator: "Welcome Spirit Life that will one day be our Future: The Unborn! We acknowledge your presence today. Future Beings, we promise to invest in creating the greatest conditions for optimal living on the planet. We pledge to you that these future fathers, grandfathers, Great- Great grandfathers will establish a powerful legacy for you to inherit and pass on for generations to come. Future Ascendants, your attendance here today will help us envision where we desire to go. We will continue to work and remain steadfast with your presence at the core of our hearts and minds."

Ritual Facilitator Pours Water

Village Responds: *"Ashe'"*

Why we are here today? The Call:

Once the elder grants permission and the Libation ritual is performed, the lead *Jegna* will set the stage by making "The Call."

The following is a reminder of the key components when making the call:

- Articulate the vision, mission, and rationale for an initiation rite, particularly in the 21st Century. Explain what the assignment will be for our time together.

- Convey to the boys, young men, their families, and communities that by accepting this they are invested in identifying, claiming, and living from the most authentic expression of their gifts and developing purpose.

- Examine the question, "why rites of passage for boys and young men of African, Indigenous and Latinx Ancestry?"

- Inform the community about the expectations of this initiation and their role in helping to support the young men during the rites process.

- Describe who our boys and young men will be upon completing the rite of passage experience. What knowledge, skills and values will they possess? How will our community be stronger after their initiation?

The Lead *Jegna* or a designee *Jegna* will be assigned to make the call to the community. The following is a sample call:

> *"Now that the Creator and our Ancestors are present, we call the community to witness the declaration of the initiatory process from Boyhood to Manhood. Gleaning from the wisdom of antiquity, the rites of passage were established to ensure that we build a legacy aligned with our highest ideals. Today our sons enter this journey as boys and will return as young men prepared to contribute their powerful gifts and Divine purpose to our families, community, nation, and world! Our boys who are present today are the ones that our Ancestors prayed would come to restore harmony, balance, and order in the world! We are grateful for their precious lives and that they responded to the call of our Ancestors!*

Our mission through the rites of passage process is to cultivate the brilliance in our boys and guide them to the threshold of their Divine purpose! As we speak, there is a narrative that has been normed in our society that our boys are flat lining in every area of life that represents success and adorning the gold medal in every category that represents failure! Our communities have fallen under the spell of a self-fulfilling prophecy of low to no expectations other than being monikered as the monsters of our society. Now more than ever it is essential for the age-old Indigenous process of transformation and becoming to be fully restored in our communities. Our boys must be reconnected to Sankofa narratives that affirm their identity centered on their relationship with the African and Indigenous concept of self (which consists of the Divine, the Ancestors, their people's story, rituals, healthy interaction with nature and community, and an emphasis on their physical/emotional/mental and Spiritual wellness). This indigenous notion of the self, supported by healthy education and socialization experiences will give birth to a man with the Indigenous genius of antiquity who has the capacity to master and innovate the modern world with the unique creative style that resonates in his blood memory).

Today, we call on our community to support our boys through this transformative process that will facilitate their emergence into young manhood. They will need all of you to remind and hold them accountable for the declarations that they make today. They will need you to be present with them as change can be uncomfortable. This initiation will guide them to unfamiliar dimensions of the self that occur when one is in transition. They will be moving from a place of how they once knew and understood themselves to a place of confusion, awkwardness, dissonance, and uncertainty. This liminal space often induces feelings of fear, insecurity, and doubt. As a community, we must hold space and be present with our boys and encourage them not to give up on themselves as our families and communities are depending on them to achieve young adulthood. We must be available to share vulnerable moments of our becoming narratives and how we persevered through the liminal phases of our development. Furthermore, we must support them through the trials by encouraging them to reach deep within themselves to master the ordeals that will occur through this experience. Lastly, our boys will benefit from participating in family and community rituals with you all. Through ritual, our boys will find grounding and have access to powers that they never knew existed. These powers will help to advance our family and community legacies.

As our boys embark on this journey, we recognize that they are the best of what we invest in them. Upon the completion of this phase of their journey, they will be prepared to take on leadership roles and model the virtues, skills and intelligences that are unique to our cultural ways of knowing and being. They will embody what Haki Madhubuti held as an ideal of manhood in our community as conveyed in his Book of Life poem:

Book of Life
Haki Madhubuti

You will recognize our brothers by the way they act and move throughout the world.
There will be a strange force about them,
There will be unspoken answers in them,
This will be obvious not only to you but to many.
The confidence they have in themselves and in their community will be evident in their quiet saneness.

The way they relate to women will be clean, complementary, responsible and with honesty.
The way they relate to children will be strong and soft,
Full of positive direction.

The way they relate to men will be that of questioning our position in this world, Will be one of planning for movement and change,
Will be one of working for their people.
Will be one of gaining and maintaining trust within their community,

These brothers at first will seem strange and unusual.
But this will not be the case for long.
They will train others and the discipline they display will become a way of life for many.
They know that this is difficult, but this is the life that they have chosen for themselves, for us, for life:

They will be the examples,
They will be the answers,
They will be the first line builders,
They will be the creators,
They will be the first to give up the pleasures,
They will be the first to share a value system,

They will be the workers,
They will be the scholars,
They will be the providers,
They will be the historians,
They will be the doctors, lawyers, educators, farmers, priests, and all that is needed for development and growth.
You will recognize these brothers and
THEY WILL NOT BETRAY YOU!!

The presence of high-quality young men can exist in our community if we all play a part! Please repeat after me, "I am because we are. And because we are, I AM!"

Let us work collectively to cultivate genius in our boys!
Ashe'

Charge for the Community—Keynote

Now that the vision, mission, intentions, and the call to the community has been proclaimed, it is time for a distinguished member of the village to share an aspirational message that will provide inspiration, validation for the initiation and offer a clear framework for the community to be prepared for the re-integration of the young men upon the completion of their passage. The message should affirm the healthy characteristics of the community and challenge the members to create opportunities for the young men to take on leadership roles, apprenticeships and clear systems that will help them transition back into the community with responsibilities that are aligned with their gifts and the unfolding of their ambitions.

Ideally, the speaker should be from the community or have a history of service to the community. He should embody the virtues of the community and stand as an exemplar of the character that the boys should emulate. He should be a high ranking *Jegna*. It would also be essential for him to be an effective speaker who possesses the capacity to motivate people. His voice and message must convey the hopes, dreams, struggles, victories, lexicon, symbols, Ancestral memory, and Soul of the community. He should be a living embodiment or working to live up to the vision of the "Book of Life" poem.

His talk should raise the questions: what does 21st century African or Indigenous manhood look like? What should be essential concepts, values and skills mastered to ensure that we thrive in this time (particularly in a time where the pandemic magnified needs that were neglected in society prior to the global shut down)? What do we need to do to be optimally healthy post-pandemic? How do we maintain healthy family and community relationships? How do we navigate life and build momentum to establish strong legacies while addressing the historic traumas, Persistent Traumas and Stressful Environments (PTSE)? What Healing- Centered practices do we need to engage in as families and community? What does our community look like at its highest manifestation?

The above-mentioned questions are just examples of what the Keynote Speaker should address. The *Jegnas* should identify and outline the critical issues of their communities and brainstorm the affirmative qualities and the areas that need attention, particularly as it relates to the healthy education and socialization of the boys and young men.

Introduction of the *Jegna* Aspirants—Oath Statements

At this stage of the ceremony, the *Jegna* Aspirants are called to demonstrate to the community that they are ready to serve as the facilitators of this sacred process. The Lead *Jegna* will introduce each *Jegna* Aspirant and have them recite their Oath Statements. The statement should follow the framework below, yet it should not be read. During the *Jegna* Aspirant's Declaration he will share from the heart what his intentions are for serving as a facilitator. His statement should be expressed with heartfelt sincerity and integrity. Quiet, slow tempo drumming should provide acoustic aura.

Jegna Aspirant Oath Statement

I, *Jegna* Aspirant_____, have accepted the call to serve as a rites of passage facilitator. My intention for serving in this role is to_____. I have an exhibited history of _____. This experience will help support my mission as_____. Through engaging with me, the boys will learn _____. This is important for their manhood journey as it is significant for them to_____. Upon the successful completion of this rites of passage experience, I envision our boys _____.

Upon the completion of each statement, the Lead *Jegna* will request consent from the elders and affirm the *Jegna* Aspirants' participation in the initiation. The protocol should sound something like this:

> **Lead *Jegna***: "Wise Elders, *Jegna* Aspirant _____
> _____ has shared his Oath as a declaration of his
> commitment to guide our sacred rites of passage journey. Do
> you give permission for him to support our initiates in their
> manhood training process?"

> **Elders Response:** *"Ashe', Ashe', Ashe'* (Let it be so, and so it
> is – *Yoruba* language) or *Rara* (No in Yoruba)."

If the *Jegna* Aspirant has completed his initiation requirements and
has been welcomed to the ceremony, it is likely that his Oath Statement
will be accepted as he has been engaging with his mission and role as a
facilitator during his training. The only obstacle may be fear or discomfort with public speaking. If he has prepared well, his Oath Statement
will be powerful, honest, and eloquent.

To conclude this segment of the ceremony, the Lead *Jegna* will
place the Akoben necklace around the newly inducted *Jegna's* neck and
welcome him into the official role as a *Jegna*. The Lead Jegna will excitedly state to the community, "we now acknowledge our *Jegnas* who will
serve as facilitators and guides for the 20__ __ Rites of Passage Manhood Journey. The audience will applaud and say, *"Ashe', Ashe', Ashe'*!!!!"

Introduction of the Parents—Oath Statements and Introduction of the Initiates:

We are now at the stage of the ceremony where the parents and/or
guardians introduce themselves and their sons to the community. It
is at this point that the parents/guardians formally agree to have their
sons initiated into young manhood. This process is represented by the
severing of the umbilical cord, which is symbolic of separating the
boy from the world of darkness and his incorporation into the world
of light. Severance also represents the initiate's separation from the
mother, father, and the home. As the cord is cut it indicates that the
boy has entered the threshold where he will be tested and charged to
seek insight and vision.

One of the new *Jegnas* will guide the family to the podium where they will present their sons. The son will be between his parents/guardians and the *Jegna* will tie the mother and son with twine. The following is a framework for how the families will introduce themselves and their sons:

Greetings! My name is _____. In the Spirit of our Ancestors from the _____ (name the bloodline Ancestors from the mother and father's lineages), we are here to present our son, _____ (state your son's name) to the community. It is time for _____ to enter the next chapter of his life and embrace the journey to young manhood. This letter reflects the boy that he has been and the man that we envision him becoming (See Letter to Our Son – see pages 43-45)

If the letters are too long, an alternative is to have the parents respond to the following prompts and present the letter as a scroll to their son:

Parents Present Son to the Community:

I AM THE PROUD PARENT/GUARDIAN OF

_____

As my son is preparing to enter young manhood, our greatest hope for him is to…

Up to this stage of life our son, _____ has been…
It is now time for him to challenge himself to …

As his parents/guardians, we support his initiation and commit to…

Upon the completion of his rites process, we expect _____ _____ to…

After the letter is read, a *Jegna* will affirm, "A boy has left your home, a young man will return." The father will cut the twine and provide him with a medicine bag (symbolic of the expectation that he will learn his powers and Divine purpose) and his mom will offer him a sip of water (symbolic of the sustenance needed for his journey). The community will respond by saying, *Ashe', Ashe', Ashe'*!!!

Lunch Served/Musical Presentations/Visual Images of Rites Passage

At this time, the community will be good and hungry! The lunch served should be donated by the parents, *Jegnas* or other community members who will be in attendance. If this is not possible, there should be a plan to hire a caterer who specializes in the traditional meals of the cultures that are represented in the community. Also, it is important that there are a variety of options to accommodate all community members' dietary preferences (omnivores, vegetarians, and vegans).

As the Ancestors of the families and community have been intentionally summoned to be a part of the celebration, it is important to prepare a plate for them as a symbolic representation of their attendance and to be intentional about ensuring that they are being welcomed as valuable members of the ceremony. The Ancestral presence is as significant and necessary as all the physically living members, as their attendance helps to support the integrity of the ceremony as well as the intelligence and wisdom that they bring for intentions to be actualized.

To create a nice ambience during lunch, it would be valuable to have a live band, or a DJ perform. The music should be an expression of the heart and soul of the cultural taste of the communities in attendance. The music should factor in the inter-generational participants and include songs that elders, adults, young adults, and children can relate to and connect with. The music of classical artists of the cultures in attendance should be played in a heavy rotation during lunch and any other transitional periods in the ceremony.

Lastly, it would be great to create a slide show that visually displays the maturation of the boys from infancy to pre-adolescence. Other images to consider would be pictures of Indigenous groups' initiations, pictures of the *Jegna* Aspirant Initiation and other visuals that express the affirmative life of the community.

Initiate Oath Statements

It is now the moment that we have all been waiting for: the initiate Oath Statements. The initiates will make their Oath Statements and set their intentions for fully committing to the rites of passage journey.

As the Lead *Jegna* calls the initiate to the podium to make his declaration, the *Jegnas* will cleanse him with sage as a symbolic purification and entry through a portal to a new chapter. This ritual is well known in many Indigenous cultures. The smoke from the sage helps release any negative energy or illness from the energy field of a person or space.

As the boys are about to embark on their rites of passage experience, the sage ritual will ensure that they will be intentional about being impeccable with their words and conveying heart-inspired statements:

I AM A YOUNG MAN OF THE PAST

LIVING IN THE PRESENT

MOVING TOWARDS THE FUTURE

MY NAME IS _____,
the son of _____.

In honor of _____ I, _____
_____, make a commitment to ……..

I also devote myself to upholding the attitudes and behaviors of _____.

I take this oath to fulfill my vision as a_____

_____

At this stage of my life, manhood means_____

_____

The Rites of Passage experience will provide me with the opportunity to nurture my gifts and challenge my fears. During this process, you will be able to count on me for_____

_____

As I prepare for the Rites of Passage Journey, I am feeling

_____

As a representative of my family and community, I know that I am expected to_____

Upon completion of this phase of my Rites of Passage, my brothers, *Jegnas* and family will remember me for _____

_____

In the same manner as the *Jegna* Aspirant Oath, upon the completion of each statement, the Lead *Jegna* will request consent from the elders and community to affirm the initiate's participation in the Rites of Passage journey. The protocol should sound something like this:

Lead *Jegna*: Wise Elders and beloved community members, Initiate _____.
_____ has shared his Oath as a declaration of his commitment to fully engage in the Rites of Passage journey. Has _____earned the privilege to be initiated by the *Jegnas* of the _____ _____ (name the community)?

Elders and Community Response: *Ashe', Ashe', Ashe'* (Let it be so, and so it is–Yoruba) or *Rara* (No in Yoruba)

Do you grant permission for him to begin his young manhood training process?

Elders and Community Response: *Ashe', Ashe', Ashe'* (Let it be so, and so it is – Yoruba) or *Rara* (No in Yoruba)

Charge to the new Initiates: To close the ceremony, have a young man who personifies the virtues and has exhibited a commitment to upholding the ideals that the community values, offer a charge to the new initiates. This young man can be someone who has successfully been through the initiation or if this is the first Rites of Passage in the community, select a young man who exhibits leadership qualities and contributes to the affirmative advancement of the community. The brief charge should reinforce the value of the initiation and offer advice on the mindset and Spirit required to endure pain and overcome fears. The young man should share aspects of his personal narrative on his journey to "Becoming." He should also share what young manhood looks like in the community that they reside in.

Closing Words: As the induction ceremony comes to an end, the Lead *Jegna* or an Elder should emphasize and reinforce that the young men experiencing this passage are embarking on a transformative experience that will position the child to enter manhood with clarity of purpose, commitment to excellence, an upstanding character, courage, and a consciousness to contribute to their families, community, people, and world. The young men will be legacy builders.

The Lead *Jegna* or an Elder should share the above-mentioned final words. The closing should reflect on what the ceremony represents and reiterate the role that each member has in supporting the boys in their journey to young manhood.

The final words can be shared as a prayer, poem, or any form of creative expression.

Lastly, the Lead *Jegna* will close with a call and response mantra. The following is a recommended mantra that I adapted from Listervelt Middleton's poem, "On the Origin of Things":

"Sharpen your eyes.

Tune your ears.

So, you know what you see.

Understand what you hear.

Minute by minute

Hour by hour

As we know Our Story

We know Our Power!!!

Ashe', Ashe', Ashe'

Drum and Dance Closing Recession: The Elders will lead the exit procession out followed by the *Jegnas*, the initiates, the families, and the community. The drummers will play an up-tempo celebration rhythm as everyone exits.

Chapter Two

THE RITUALS

"Where ritual is absent the young ones are restless or violent, there are no real elders, and the grown-ups are bewildered. The future is dim."

—*Malidoma Patrice Some'*
Ritual: Power, Healing and Community

As a *Jegna* of the Rites of Passage journey, it is important to understand that the rituals are the most essential part of this journey. Rites of Passage is synonymous with Rituals of Passage. In the transformative initiation process, it is ritual that helps the *Jegnas* and initiates prioritize their intentions, focus, and direct the events that will occur. Rituals provide the accessing points to receive clear instructions and direction from the Indwelling intelligences (Spirit), the Ancestors, the Elemental forces and guides that support the Rites of Passage experience. Rituals provide information that supports the internalization of the knowledge, virtues and skills that will be mastered during the initiation. Also, Indigenous rituals help communities remember the cultural technology that has been lost in modern society. They help communities restore knowledge that cultivates an organic way of knowing and being. As the Rites of Passage process is designed to challenge initiates to cross through thresholds and enter the unknown, rituals help to quell the ego and make the mind, body, and Spirit available to the sensibilities that are being summoned to emerge.

Ritual brings order, importance, context and focus to our lives. It aligns our intention with our actions, and it sets the stage for the action to be as effective as possible. Ritual grounds us in the present; it rescues us from dwelling on the past and worrying about the future. Rituals help to internalize our call to purpose by formalizing ideals, revealing our gifts, and aligning our purpose to address the needs of our community. Rituals are:

- ⚜ "A prescribed set of actions that set the stage for a powerful experience." —Chike Akua, *Honoring Our Ancestral Obligations*
- ⚜ Are actions with intentional symbolic meaning undertaken for a specific cultural purpose. —Chegg.com

Ritual: a stylized expression of a community's values, commitments, and beliefs.

The First World Alliance Lecture Series

At the age of thirteen, my journey guided me to institutions, organizations and spaces that would help me cultivate an identity that was centered on concepts and practices aimed at enlightening people of African Ancestry about the "Know Thyself" path. At the age of seventeen, I attended what would become a life transformative experience that helped to launch my mission as a cultural custodian, educator, vehicle for healing and Indigenous Spiritual practitioner.

The First World African Alliance Lecture Series was an institution that hosted the premiere African Centered scholars, thinkers, artists, activists, and practitioners. They provided a narrative that was rooted in African and Indigenous frameworks geared to free the African mind from the self-effacing and destructive damage that a Eurocentric education and socialization produces. It was here that I was exposed to the greatest scholars of the last quarter of the 20th century who were charged with the mission of penetrating the thick corrosion that miseducation, White media, European religions, and the socialization under White Supremacy produces. The First World Lecture Series was a sacred space that helped people of African Ancestry re-imagine who we are by providing a people's narrative that is not found in schools, churches or institutions deeply seeped in Eurocentric thought. According to Minister Clemson Brown, founder of the United Afrikan Movement (U.A.M.), *"The First World Alliance was a living, spiritual forum that provided an international education foundation for Afrikan people. It was a place where scholars from all over the world disseminated the knowledge, research, and experiences of our ancient and present times."* *(Hiphopwired.com)*

The internalization of White Supremacy reinforced by all systems in America sets people of African and Indigenous Ancestry up for self-hatred and self-destructive behaviors that sabotage our best interest and serve the priorities and concerns of "Whiteness." My Spirit yearned to fill the void of knowing that I was here for a greater purpose and that there was something that I was missing to activate my indwelling powers. Learning my people's narrative and being exposed to people who were awakened to the knowledge of themselves helped me to cultivate a new way of thinking, knowing and being that would contribute to identifying, claiming, and living what would become my calling to serve my community as a guide and a bridge to the greatest version of ourselves. The exposure to powerful modern day *Djelis* (Keepers of our sacred stories) like Dr. Asa Hilliard, Dr. John Henrick Clarke, Dr. Leonard Jefferies, Dr. Francis Cress Welsing, Dr. Adelaide Sandford, Professor James Small, Dr. Ivan Van Sertima, Dr. Marimba Ani, Dr. Wayne Chandler, Dr. Khalid Abdul Muhammad, Dr. Amos Wilson, Dr. Na'im Akbar, Sister Souljah, Dr. Molefi Asante, Listervelt Middleton, Dr. Jacob Carruthers, Dr. Yosef Ben Yochannan, Dr. Wade Nobles, Kwame Touré and others would serve as my great awakening and ushered in the next chapter of my passage as a Rites of Passage practitioner.

These powerful scholars, activists, cultural warriors, and practitioners enlightened me to an identity that helped to raise the expectations that I had for myself personally and academically. The more that I learned about my people's narrative the more supported I felt in building confidence and taking risks to cross thresholds that I never imagined I would enter. The potent information delivered by the presenters in a cultural style that felt like home, helped me to integrate and internalize Indigenous African thoughts, frameworks, and practices.

Equally as powerful as the presentations was the opening ritual that would start every session. To set the stage for the lectures, the ritual leader would open with an acknowledgement of the elders, the children and African life. Also, a statement that would identify the current condition of people of African Ancestry would be read. The statement was like what occurs in the Alcoholics Anonymous 12-Step Program, which is an admission to being an addict. In the declaration of the First World Ritual, the participants collectively acknowledged that we were oppressed under European hegemony. The ritual leader would then speak about our glorious past that extended beyond our interaction with European conquerors and bring us up to date on our current dilemma and what it would take to free ourselves from the residue of our enslavement, colonization, and the reality of being oppressed. The following is the opening ritual for the First World Alliance:

> **Ritual Leader:** "Hotep! In praise of African Gods and Goddesses. In the tradition of our Ancestors and in celebration of our history. We of the First World invite you to join us in our opening ritual."
>
> "To honor our elders, for those Africans who are 60 years of age or older please stand."
>
> **Participants:** Applaud

Ritual Leader: "To African Elders"

Ritual Leader: "To honor our children, those among us and those who have left us, would the youngest African child in the house please stand or be held up."

Participants: Applaud

Ritual Leader: "To African Children"

Ritual Leader: "To honor African life, would those sisters carrying a child in their sacred womb please stand. If the father is present, please stand."

Participants: Applaud

Ritual Leader: "To our Brothers and Sisters who are joining us for the first time, would you please stand so that we can welcome you into our African family."

Participants: Applaud

Ritual Leader: *"Medasi – Asante Sana."* (Thank you in Twi and Kiswahili)

The next part of the ritual was the reading of two of Listervelt Middleton's (journalist, producer, scholar, and poet) poems, "On the Origin of Things" and "War Horn." The poems were read by community participants who were requested to share in the ritual. Both poems conveyed affirmative messages about the essence of our glorious past and the cultural retentions that are a continuum that live in our practices today. These poems spoke to the *soul of Blackness* and called us to claim and live from our rich heritage. The poems helped to set the stage for the presenters to execute their mission with a commitment to cultural excellence and for the participants to be present and open to learning the deep wisdom of their Ancestors.

The following are the poems that were shared:

"On the Origin of Things"
Listervelt Middleton

Look around you Black Child
Your creation is everywhere.
Though painted, distorted, given new names
They bear your prints just the same.

So, sharpen your eyes.
Tune your ear.
So, you know what you see.
Understand what you hear.

You were the first to write.
The first to read.
Humanity sprang from your Black seed.
For 110,00 years you were here alone
And then the Caucasian man was born.
Behind the ice, inside the cold
A chill set in this new man's soul
Other minds have been credited with the things they learned
from you.
Newton, Pythagoras, Kepler, and Galileo too

Sharpen your eyes.
Tune your ear.
So, you know what you see.
Understand what you hear.

You made the serpent the symbol of the healing arts.
and African Justice was Goddess Ma'at
Who weighed herself against the African Soul?
Truth and Justice blindfold
The George Washington Monument is yours too.
a copy of the African Tekenu
A symbol of the Black Worlds powers of Creation
The Black man's penis in Divine procreation
The King of Southern Egypt wore the White Crown
Keep listening and you'll catch your mouth.
When you learn that the Central Government in Egypt was
known as the White House

Sharpen your eyes.
Tune your ears.
So, you know what you see.
Understand what you hear.

Your God Osiris was restored to life.
Long before Buddha, long before Christ
And today what you call Madonna and child.
Is but the first Black family worshipped 'long the Nile.
And when you feel the Spirit - the Holy Ghost
You should know it started at Abydos.
Where God Osiris' body was laid
The holy land where Africans prayed.

Minute by minute
Hour by hour

As you lose your history
You lose your power.

So, sharpen your eyes.
Tune your ears.
So, you know what you see.
Understand what you hear

Listervelt Middleton
"The War Horns"

Listen to the horns.
The war horns calling, calling the people.
to battle
Calling the people
to the Gods of our Ancestors...
Calling the people to Afrikan Gods
Calling the people to Amma, Olodumare, Ausar, Auset
Calling our image makers:
Romeare Bearden, Elizabeth Catlett
to mount scaffold and like the Netcher (God) Shu,
rise again to heaven.
Afrikan female form
to its rightful place in the ceilings of our holy places
Calling
Calling the people to arms
With brushes and paint to spray
their stained-glass churches
With new images of self
New images of divinity

No minstrel god
No white god in black face
Calling
Calling the people to Afrikan theology
Past imitation and cooptation
Past the seductive attraction of
Bibles, Korans, and robes covered and draped.
with kente cloth
Calling the people to Afrikan spirituality
to Ancestor Communion
Calling the people to the mortuary meal
To the funeral supper
To break bread with the body-soul
in spiritual unity
(Break the chains from the drums
and let them speak again!
Let them beat
again!
In the dance of joy and resurrection)
listen to the horns!
Calling
Calling the people
to worship at our sacred places
Calling the people to Abydos
to Ile-Ife
Calling the people back across
the Isthmus of Suez,
The Bering Strait,
to the Great Lakes,

to the first cemetery
where Kamoya Kimeu
walked and exhumed our Ancestors.
For Leakey and European science
Calling
Calling the children away from chimneys
red stockings and European mythology
Calling the children to build for us
what elves and white helpers will not
Calling the children
Calling the people to Kwanzaa, to Crop over, to Junkanoo.
Calling the people to Afrikan wisdom
Calling our black smiths
Calling Philip Simmons
to design new quotation marks
of reverence
New MDW NETCHER (hieroglyphs)
of steel
Burn them on our chests,
Hang them in the sky.
Around our proverbs and sacred writings
Around the Book of Coming Forth by Day
Around the teachings of Ptah-Hotep
Fanon, Terence Afer, Robeson, Fannie Lou
Grandma and Grandpa
And let the moon be a PERIOD in the heavens.
Listen to the horns.
Calling
Calling the people
to ARMS

These powerful poems, particularly "On the Origin of Things," impacted my life deeply. I began to incorporate "On the Origin of Things" into my personal rituals and it supported my journey to live from the expectations, intentions, and commitments that my Ancestors established. As a student at Hampton University, I would start my day with an invocation, meditation, and the reading of Middleton's poem. I began to experience more confidence in my intellect and code of ethics. As I participated in class, I grew more trusting in my ability to provide counter narratives and respectfully challenged the professors on historical perspectives that were seeped in Eurocentric thought. I also began to cultivate my voice as a leader and sought opportunities to speak and share my growing leadership platform. This was a major shift for me as I was shy and feared public speaking. Cultivating my voice through my daily recitation of the "On the Origin of Things" aligned me to the brilliance of my Ancestors and allowed for their presence to be a part of my next chapter as a young educator and leader.

Once I internalized the poem, I began to lead community rituals that incorporated the poem. "On the Origin of Things" became a part of my being and I attribute it to the pillars that have been essential to the ritual practice that I facilitate to this day. As an educator, Rites of Passage leader and Ritual Facilitator, I have creatively co-designed rituals that have been adapted to bring this poem into the process of the identity transformation of thousands of Rites facilitators and initiates. This poem has been the impetus that drives our educational and socialization experiences with the mission of re-imagining and restoring our lives with the brilliance of our Ancestors at the core. I attribute to Middleton's classically scribed "On the Origin of Things" the success of the institutions and organizations that have participated in the rituals, and the boys and young men who have restored identity and internalized this poetic narrative.

Walk of Transformation Ceremonial Procession at the
Eagle Mentoring Summit Eagle Academy for Young Men, Bronx, NY, 2019
Credit for photograph – Matthew Fuego, Mat Media.

UAAHC Ritual

As the co-founder of the Urban Assembly Academy of History and Citizenship for Young Men (UAAHC), we placed high value on the rituals that we facilitated. All our schoolwide gatherings were summoned by the call of the drums. In fact, the drum was used in place of the school bell and echoed through the halls as our scholars were transitioning to their next classes. Our schoolwide events would begin with Libations that were customized for the purpose of our gatherings (See pp. 33-34 for review*)*. Libations were followed by call and responses, words of wisdom, affirmations, and Middleton's "Sharpen Your Eyes" mantra. Below is the ritual that I designed and facilitated at the school (UAAHC) that I co-founded in the South Bronx. It was inspired by the rituals that were conceived by the first Rites of Passage program (Harambee Rites of Passage Group) that my older brother (Dr. RA Ptahsen Shabazz) and I launched in the

Greenburgh, NY community in which we were raised. The intention was to help the boys that we were serving to internalize the core principles of our organization (*Nguzo Saba*—Seven Principles of Kwanzaa) and call on the Divine and the Ancestors to support our initiation process. It was also facilitated to activate the indwelling gifts, intelligences, and mission so that the boys would be fully present to learn with their Indigenous sensibilities charged and fully present. This ritual was also inspired by my athletic journey. The intention was to create a process that cultivated the same Warrior energy that boys and young men take on the court, field, track or wherever they have identified as their domain to test their physical, mental, emotional, and Spiritual gifts. The objective was to summon the powers that called on their mission and authentic voices to be present, ready, and available to perform at their highest capacity in the classroom.

At UAAHC, we witnessed the amazing sense of community and brotherhood that existed when we participated in school wide rituals. During assemblies, our Libations, call and response mantras, affirmations and community celebrations anchored us in our core values and there was a collective interest to be able to experience this incredible power daily. Our dilemma was that we shared a building with five other schools and space was limited. We needed a consistent space that we could meet daily, invoke the energy, and create the ambience that set a strong intention for the day. When we finished exhausting all the excuses and grew weary of exploring the ideal space, we decided to declare our hallway as the sacred space where our community ritual would occur. Once we informed the other schools about our vision, we received some pushback as the other learning communities were concerned about how the sound might disrupt the beginning of their classes. Yet we were successful in convincing the reluctant school leaders and once we performed our first 3rd Period Ritual, we knew we had opened the way for optimal levels of community engagement.

The ritual opened with the drum call. A cohort of scholars who were "called" by the Djembe took the responsibility to set the drums up prior to the ritual. They were charged to play some of the traditional rhythms that they learned from me and other cultural custodians that were connected to our learning community. As the drums reached exhilarating heights, we played the break to stop the rhythm and immediately went into our call and response chant. The following is the *UAAHC* 3rd period ritual that occurred daily:

Libation

Call: "What time is it?"
Response: "*UAAHC* Time!" (Recite two times)

Call: "Brothers are we ready?"
Response: "*UAAHC* Ready!" (Recite two times)

Call: "Who are we?"
Response: "Men of the past, living in the present, moving towards the future." (Recite two times)

Call: "What hood we rep?"
Response: "Manhood!"

Call: "What hood we rep?"
Response: "Brotherhood" (Recite 2 times)

Call: "I want for my brother…"
Response: "What I want for myself" (Recite 2 times)

Call: "Retrieve the past"
Response: "Create the future" (Recite 2 times)

Call: "Sharpen your eyes.
    Tune your ears.
    So, you know what you see.
    Understand what you hear."

Response: "Minute by minute

Hour by hour

As we know Our Story

We know Our POWER!!!

Everyone: *UAAHC*!!!!!

Upon the completion of the call and response, we proceeded with a quote for the week and an affirmation for the day. After that, we celebrated our scholars during what we called Warrior Acknowledgements (the Warrior was our totem/mascot). Warrior Acknowledgements were public offerings of accolades and praise for academic accomplishments and exhibiting of our core values (Unity, Self-Determination, Collective Work and Responsibility, Cooperative Economics, Purpose, Creativity and Faith). Our scholars were recognized for their achievements and often gifted with symbols that reflected their growth and new status within our community.

Next, we would make announcements that informed our young scholars of upcoming events, opportunities and other significant information that contributed to their journey as scholars, brothers and developing young men! Lastly, we closed out with the powerful "Sharpen your eyes..." (Adapted from Listervelt Middleton's poem) mantra.

The UAAHC rituals were designed to harness the powers of a forgotten legacy, celebrate the present and affirm a powerful future. Each day we envisioned and re-imagined a world where we were victorious and had access to the indwelling powers and tools that ushered us all to greater possibilities. A well-crafted ritual will feel as if the experience was designed specifically with a message in mind for an individual. We would often receive responses from our scholars and teachers that the quote or affirmation was exactly what someone was thinking or what they needed to hear.

Additionally, on certain days (Monday and Friday), we collectively recited literature that aligned to our school's mission. As a school that was designed to cultivate the genius of boys and young men of

African and Latino Ancestry, we intentionally ritualized narrating ideals that reinforced the vision of what optimal expressions of manhood looked like from our people's perspective. Our community declaring these virtues served as a constant reminder of the mindset, habit and daily behaviors that would align us to our Ancestral obligations and the expectations of what it meant to be a Scholar Warrior. Moreover, the staff and scholars were encouraged to write poems, declarations, monologues, and creative illustrations that aligned with our core values, and we would include these original creative expressions in our rituals. The following represents some of our standard passages that were infused into our rituals:

UAAHC Seven Core Principles (Adapted from the *Nguzo Saba* View *the African American Holiday of Kwanzaa-Karenga*):

Unity: to strive for and maintain unity within the family, community, school, and our people.

Self Determination: to give scholars and educators the capacity to define and create themselves.

Collective Work and Responsibility: to empower scholars and educators to take a proactive role in community affairs.

Cooperative Economics: to encourage scholars and educators to share resources for the betterment of their community.

Purpose: to help scholars and educators identify and claim their strengths to make a positive contribution to society.

Creativity: to cultivate one's imagination through artistic modes of expression.

Faith: to strengthen scholars and educators' confidence in their ability to achieve excellence.

"Book of Life" Poem by Haki Madhubuti

UAAHC Scholar Creed

I am a UAAHC Scholar.

In my actions, words, and deeds I journey the path of a Warrior.

When I am present, I exude brilliance, character, and awesome power.

Just look at my impeccable attire.

Prepared for my rendezvous with destiny, I take full advantage of all opportunities.

Like the Sankofa Bird, I reached back for my legacy, ushering in a new reality.

The Nguzo Saba-the keys to unlock the mysteries to building community.

Each breath of my life, I create a rich history.

I pledge with my entire being to live with self-love, respect, and integrity.

Today, I claim victory over the forces that attempt to destroy me.

I possess self-control, moving towards self-mastery.

Executing my educational master plan, I am striving to become a responsible UAAHC man.

—Kamau Ptah, *Co-founder*
Urban Assembly Academy of History and
Citizenship for Young Men (UAAHC)

Our Deepest Fear

"Our deepest fear is not that we are inadequate. Our deepest fear is that we are powerful beyond measure. It is not our light, not our darkness, that most frightens us. We ask ourselves, "Who am I to be brilliant, gorgeous, talented, and fabulous?" Who are you not to be? You are a child of God. You playing small doesn't serve the world. There's nothing enlightened about shrinking so that other people won't feel insecure around you. We are all meant to shine, as children do. We are born to make manifest the glory of God that is within us. It's not just in some of us, it's in everyone. And as we let our own light shine, we unconsciously give other people permission to do the same. As we are liberated from our own fear, our presence automatically liberates others."

—Marianne Williamson,
A Return to Love, 1992

From Maleness to Manhood

"Males are capable of sight-seeing. As reality moves by, they observe it from a distance with a hand extended, hoping for a handout. Boys have dreams. They dream, they think, they wonder, they build unreal worlds in their minds. Only men have visions and visions become the instrument of human collective societal transformation. If you want to be who you are, then become a man and the world will be transformed by you."

—Dr. Naim Akbar
Visions for Black Men

Components of a Community Ritual

As you are designing a ritual it is essential that you operate with a framework, yet do not be too rigid. There are opportunities to be in the moment but if you are too attached to the script, the inspiration from the Divine, the Elements and Ancestors can be blocked from expressing something necessary for the occasion, that needs to be communicated. . The role of the ritual leader is that of a medium. The ritualist is the bridge to connecting the intentions of the ritual with the participants and the Divine Powers that are helping to support the success and optimal outcomes of the event. The following are some of the key components to facilitating an effective ritual:

- ✤ **Clear Intention:** Be clear about the purpose of the ritual. What do you want to achieve in the moment and beyond? What has the community been called to accomplish? What type of Spirit and qualities does the collective group need to possess to achieve the principles that are the pillars of the community? What intelligences are necessary for the collective to live in alignment with the call? What guides or exemplars should be summoned to support the objectives of the event? Who are we as a collective upon the completion of our ritual and what value will our ritual be for ourselves, our families, communities, and world?

- ✤ **Sacred Space**: In preparation for the ritual, it is important to create a safe, clean and Spirit imbued environment. If possible, burn sage, myrrh with frankincense, palo santo or copal. These aromatic elements help to purify the space and clean any toxic energies that may be lingering. If you are in a space that does not permit the burning of these elements, you can spray liquid sage to cleanse the energy. If possible, create an altar (centerpiece) that includes the elemental forces (fire, air, water, minerals, earth, and nature). These elements help to support and transform the releasing of undesirable outcomes and serve as portals to attract information and messages from the unseen realms. Additionally, you may place on the altar symbols that represent the virtues of the community, desired community outcomes, and images of the Ancestors of community participants.

- ✤ **Acknowledgement of community members:** Community members (living or Ancestral) who have embodied the community ideals and commitments should be recognized and honored. It is important to highlight the behaviors that help to affirm community norms as a method of acknowledging what healthy living looks like and celebrate those who are living up to the community's ethical codes.

🦋 **Community Voice:** The ritual leader should create opportunities for community members to participate in the ritual. The voices of the community members contribute to the multiple ways that the mission, virtues, and individual gifts can be expressed. Some of the ways to involve other members would be for them to set up the space for the ritual, pour Libations, lead the call and response, recite a poem aligned to the mission, offer gratitude to other community members, read the quote of the day, lead the affirmation, drum, respond to the call and responses, and clean up the space after the ritual is complete. Through modeling the ritual practices, the ritual leader will facilitate with a powerful verve, presence, and with elevated levels of emotional intention as it is said that the Universe responds to passionate feeling invocations.

🦋 **Music (Particularly Live Acoustic):** Music creates the ambience, frequency and the portal that activates the opportunity for crossing thresholds. Drums, flutes, mbiras, tambourines, bells, and other acoustic instruments help to create the atmosphere for harmony, balance, and order. It supports the ritual's intent and provides heart-centered messaging that generates the verve for creativity, imagination, and movement (mental, physical, emotional, and Spiritual). The learning of indigenous songs and rhythms that support the intention of optimal community living would be beneficial for powerful ritual experiences. The musicians should be mindful of intent and approach the ritual as clear-mindedly as possible as their energy is influencing the ritual. Lastly, the music should be inspired and influenced by the core values of the community and serve as the rhythmic soundtrack for the community's ideals.

🦋 **Powerful Closing:** The ritual should end with an expression of gratitude for the powerful presence of the entire community, including the Divine and the Ancestors that supported the intention of the ritual. There should be a final charge to the community that reinforces the objectives of the exercise and calls on the attributes needed to achieve the vision conveyed for the ritual. The Ritual Leader should provide assurance that the ritual was successful and encourage the community to walk with a Spirit of expectancy with full awareness that the summons was received and that all that was expressed will manifest.

Ritual is a significant process for establishing the optimal expression of community. In many Indigenous and African cultures, it is agreed that "A community that does not have a ritual cannot exist." (Somé, *Crossroads: The Quest for Contemporary Rites of Passage*)

Closing Ritual
2012 Coalition of Schools Educating Boys of Color Gathering
of Leaders Young Men's Passage Durham, North Carolina

Trial—Crafting the Rituals:

- What personal rituals do you practice daily? Why?
- For each daily ritual that you perform, what is your intention?

- What does your ritual give you access to and how does it impact your day?

- Reflect on the community rituals that you have participated in your life experiences.

- Based on the vision of your rites of passage initiation for the boys, what type of rituals do you think are essential to achieve the outcomes that the community collectively desires?

- Lead the group through one of your personal rituals and share the intention, rationale, and the impact of this ritual in your life.

- Using the components of a community ritual, create an opening and closing ritual for the rites of passage group that factors in the vision, mission, and core values of the community.

CHAPTER THREE

THE TRIALS

"Every positive change - every jump to a higher level of energy and awareness - involves a rite of passage. Each time to ascend to a higher rung on the ladder of personal evolution, we must go through a period of discomfort, of initiation. I have never found an exception."

—*Dan Millman*
Living on Purpose

For many people, the Rites of Passage Ceremony is often associated with the entire initiation. The ceremony starts and culminates the formal Rites of Passage initiation, yet there are other critical phases that are germane to the process. To arrive at the ceremony there are trials that must be overcome to earn the privileges and responsibilities of the new status that one achieves through initiation. Earning privileges and responsibilities comes with overcoming obstacles, proving yourself worthy of having status and being equipped with the knowledge, skills, intelligences, sensibilities, values, and powers gained through mastery of the trials.

Trials are ordeals that are centered on solving problems, testing skills, and building one's capacity to make decisions that are culturally and ethically centered. In a formal and structured Rites of Passage, the trials are designed to disorient and disrupt the initiates' immature way of knowing and being. The *Jegnas* intentionally choreograph trials that completely take the initiates out of their comfort zone. At the core of all the trials is a test to endure pain (physical, mental, and emotional) and confront fear. These two threshold tests are opportunities for the emergence of a new awareness and the awakening of dormant qualities.

Trauma and Isolation

The trial phase begins with trauma and isolation – an event that abruptly uproots the initiate from their normal everyday routines and norms. This orchestrated traumatic experience serves as a shock that unexpectedly jolts the initiate and jump starts the initiation. Many will recall the classic movie, *Roots* (based on the novel written by Alex Haley), where Kunta Kinte was abducted by the elders of his Mandingo clan. One of the *Jegnas* (known as Kintango in the Mandingo ethnic group) unexpectedly placed a burlap sack over Kunta's head and guided him to the other boys in his village who also experienced the same traumatic process. The boys were lined up with the sack on their heads and marched miles to a remote area in the woods to begin their rites process. As Kunta's mother observed this traditional process, she affirmed, "a boy has left the village, a man will return."

The feeling of being isolated occurs when the initiate recognizes that he is far removed from the daily comforts of family and community. He is forced to begin the process of thinking and making decisions based on his own intelligence that were influenced by his education, socialization, and family/community values. Keep in mind that the initiate thinks and processes life as a child and the rites training is designed to support his transition to adulthood. He will learn the value of his unique contribution to his family and community based on the needs of his people and the collective narrative that defines their identity. He will identify his purpose and gifts and learn how to use them for the advancement of his culture and society.

Young man testing his pain threshold during a martial arts trial
2018 Annual Eagle Academy Mentoring Summit Bronx, NY
Credit for photograph – Matthew Fuego, Mat Media.

The Best Talk in Town—Traumatic Journey to Cultivate Voice:

It was 1987, my senior year of high school and I was a part of the Woodlands Individualized Senior Experience (WISE), a program that permits students an opportunity to design and implement their self-directed projects during their senior year. After contemplating the type of internship that I wanted to explore, I decided to pursue education. Several days out of the week, I served as a Teacher Assistant supporting first grade students with their academic assignments and social and emotional needs. I was assigned to support my third-grade teacher (teaching first grade at this time) who I was fond of as a student. As an intern exploring the teaching profession, I was keenly aware that one of my trials would be to cultivate my voice as I was quiet and a shy child and young man. As a part of my responsibilities, I was gradually confronting my reticent nature as I had to communicate with other educators and the children that I assisted. There was one traumatic event that occurred during the WISE journey that put me on an intentional path to a self-motivated initiation aimed at cultivating my voice.

It started out as a typical day for me as I attended my regular classes. We would be leaving school early to attend a field trip to one of my classmate's WISE Internship; her project was with WPIX Television Network. Our mission was to participate in a talk show, entitled *The Best Talk in Town*. Our discussion was centered on racism in the New York Metropolitan area. During this time, there were growing incidents occurring with police brutality, assaults and murders of Black people, particularly Black boys and men in the New York Tri-State area. The racial tension was escalating, and violent confrontations and attacks on Black people were becoming a focus of concern. The most infamous fatal events that occurred in the 1980s involved Willie Turks (1982), Eleanor Bumpers (1984), Michael Griffith (1986), and Yusef Hawkins (1989).

The most current issue that made national news during the time of the taping of *The Best Talk in Town* was the Michael Griffith incident. Michael Griffith's death occurred in Howard Beach, an Italian American community in Queens, NY. Griffith and two of his friends were driving from Brooklyn to Queens, when their car broke down near Howard Beach. They walked several miles to a pizza parlor in Howard Beach, where they asked to use a phone to call for assistance. After being told there was no phone available, they ordered some pizza. When the men left the pizzeria, a gang of White teens confronted them. Griffith, twenty-three years of age, was chased by the mob into traffic on the Belt Parkway and died after being hit by a car.

On a local and more personal level, I also had a friend who was assaulted by a White mob of college students while attending a basketball game at the State University of Potsdam. The result of the mayhem left his jaw broken. Our community was angered by this event and coupled with the headline issues that were occurring, *The Best Talk in Town* was intended to be a youth-centered forum to address the racial tensions that were arising in New York. We were present with several schools from New York City and surrounding areas to discuss our perspectives on the issues that were occurring within our communities.

I recall entering the studio and being welcomed by the hostess of the show. As we got settled, the host shared the vision and the protocols that we must adhere to for the best possible outcomes of the show. I did not intend to be vocal that day; as a personal practice, I was an observer and felt quite at home in my silence. As the show officially started, I became nervous. I began to take notice of my surroundings and recognized that this new experience was very intimidating. I immediately began to think that I should have stayed home. The host began to reflect on the incident about my friend and raised the quite simple question, "How did you feel about what occurred with your classmate?" I did not think about answering the question until I recognized the host placed the microphone in front of my mouth. My heart dropped into my stomach, my hands became sweaty, and my mouth became dry. I wanted to sprint out of the studio. I looked up at the monitor and noticed that the camera had a close-up of my face. I became ultra self-conscious at that moment. All I remember is responding to the question by repeating, "I felt…, I felt…, I felt…." I heard my nervous voice amplified loudly through the speakers in this monotone depressing mantra and I made the decision to tap out. I subtly waved my hand to let the host know that I was done. She continued to encourage me by saying "it's ok, tell us how you feel." In my mind, I said, "If you don't get this mic out my face, I'm gonna slap it across the studio." She received the body language and proceeded to my classmate, who was eager, confident and had no reservations about answering the question. For the rest of the show, I sat quietly, annoyed, and embarrassed.

As we returned home, I recalled one of my teachers attempting to cheer me up. She made mention to something like being prepared for the next time. I did not take in what she was saying yet appreciated her effort to make me feel better. One of my classmates attempted to offer her words of encouragement. She cheerfully asserted, "Don't worry about what happened! You look so good that no one is even gonna notice or care about what you had to say!" I thought to myself, "WOW…do most people see me as a shell with no substance?" Her comment cut me deep and I promised myself that the next time I opened my mouth I would have something significant to say. Yet, the only life preserver that I had to hold on to was reflecting on my grandmother's affirmative words when she would often tell me and others in my family, "My grandson doesn't have a lot to say, but when he speaks, he speaks volumes."

From that day forward, I committed myself to cultivating my voice. I found myself researching the dictionary to identify words that captured some of my deep thoughts. One of the requirements for the WISE Internship was to prepare a forty-five-minute presentation reflecting on the internship experience, personal highlights, challenges, professional knowledge learned and future goals. "Forty- five minutes! Forty-five minutes of talking," I said to myself. For me, this would be a huge mission. I devoted myself to preparing for this final presentation that would represent my final trial as a high school student. I recall spending countless hours organizing my visuals and practicing my presentation. My mother stayed up with me as I practiced with her until the late-night hours. Up to this phase of my educational experience, I had never worked harder on an assignment. I was determined to demonstrate to myself that I was more than how I perceived myself.

On the day of the presentation, I was extremely nervous, yet I was ready to put everything on the line. I called on my athletic mind-set to fully show up to this trial. I constructed in my mind that this presentation was going to usher me into a new enlightened awareness of myself. As my staff adviser introduced me, I felt my entire body pulsating. I reminded myself to breathe and focus on the people who helped to quell my anxiety. The presentation was open to the public and several of my friends, teachers, mentors and of course my mother were present to witness what would become the beginning of identifying, claiming, and expressing my voice and mission.

As I began to present, I could hear the tension in my voice. I remember after the first five minutes I noticed that the audience seemed intrigued by what I was sharing. By the time I started to present my visuals, I felt like I was owning the experience. As soon as I became comfortable in the process, one slight thought of looking for the angst created a disruption, and I lost track of the direction towards which I was heading. I quickly recovered and found my rhythm. By the time I reached the conclusion, I was feeling empowered. After my last remarks, I took a deep sigh of relief and my body felt free, relieved, and ecstatic. At that moment, it did not matter how the Question-and-Answer period went; I had accomplished what in my mind was monumental. I confronted and overcame one of my greatest fears and I affirmed that I had intellectual substance and a voice that was valuable to my community.

The trauma of having my vulnerability exposed on television was an invitation to enter the initiation that put me on a course to cultivate my voice. Though I was not in complete isolation in my quest, the mere shift of my priorities separated me from some of the activities and people with whom I would normally interface. As this journey was very personal to me and was a direct call to action, no one quite understood the quest that I was pursuing. From the outside looking in, my peer group and community were in awe of my popularity and athleticism. Very few people were challenging me to examine my blind spots or were concerned about what lived in my mind and Spirit. Deep inside my Spirit, I realized that my voice would be essential to my purpose in life. From the WISE experience, I knew that I had more work to do with developing my oratory skills and the essence of my voice. As I entered college that year, I would continue to intentionally find opportunities to confront my fear of public speaking and hone my expression.

Liminal Phase

The next stage of the trials involves the liminal ordeals. In a formal initiation, the liminal phase is designed to intentionally place an initiate in a mental and emotional state of chaos and confusion. With little that resembles what his previous life experiences were, he is now placed in a situation where he begins to recognize that he is no longer what he used to be yet has no idea what he will become. The liminal phase represents a state of being lost. The liminal phase is when the initiate is overwhelmed with all the new experiences and the barrage of challenging tests. He begins to recognize that the powers and intelligence that worked for him during his previous stage of life are serving little value to him during his trials. The initiate feels weary, confused, swamped and uncertain. His disorientation breaks him down and he begins to question his capacity to pass the trials. His frustration and mixed emotions make him feel like he is awkward and in a perpetual state of failure. During this stage he may want to give up and return to the comfort and luxury of his former status.

Navigating the Liminal: Where Is My Home?

It was 1989 and I had just completed my sophomore year of college at Hampton University. I felt accomplished as I continued to prove to myself that I could handle the rigors and demands of navigating independent living and perform academically. There were many changes occurring in my personal and family life. During my first two years at college, I began to deepen my exploration into the "Know Thyself" path. As a History/Social Science and Education Major, I immersed myself in African centered thought and practices. I devoted a lot of my studies to scholars like Dr. Na'im Akbar, Dr. Jawanza Kunjufu, Dr. Asa Hilliard, Dr. Frances Cress Welsing, Dr. Tony Martin, Dr. John Henrick Clarke, Dr. Leonard Jefferies, Professor James Smalls, Professor Kaba Hiawatha (Brother Booker T. Coleman), Dr. Molefi Asante, Dr. Wade Nobles, Dr. Jacob Carruthers, Dr. Nathan and Julia Hare, Dr. Maulana Karenga, Haki Madhubuti, Dr. Khalid Abdul Muhammad, Dr. Marimba Ani, Dr. Sinclair Drake, Kwame Touré, Dr. Vincent Harding and a host of other erudite scholar-warrior-activists.

On my Spiritual path, I began to study Islam from the teachings of the Honorable Elijah Muhammad under the leadership of the Honorable Minister Louis Farrakhan. As Islam was my anchor at that time,

I also found a powerful sense of community with the Hebrew Israelite community, which I had exposure to during my early adolescence. From the age of thirteen, I would periodically attend Shabbat services at the Bereshith Cultural Center in Mount Vernon, NY under the guidance of Kohain Nathanaya Helevi. Additionally, I was drawn to the Spiritual doctrine, meditation practices and rituals of the Nile Valley as expressed through the Ausar-Auset Society under Ra U Nefer Amen. The late 1980s presented a resurgence in African-centered philosophy and activism that was reflected in the culture of Black communities throughout America and by many young people who were envisioning a reality that reflected a more self-determined path. These ideas were also being propagated through Hip Hop music and artists like Public Enemy, X-Clan, Brand Nubians, KRS-1, Queen Latifah, Eric B and Rakim, Tribe Called Quest, Arrested Development, The Fugees, Digable Planets, Poor Righteous Teachers, Heavy D, Pete Rock and CL Smooth and the Guru to name a few. Reggae continued to convey Spiritual and socially conscious music through artists like Steel Pulse, Ziggy Marley, and the Melody Makers, Shinehead, Shabba Ranks, Gregory Isaacs, Bunny Wailer, Cocoa T, Sugar Minott, Ini Kamoze, Linton Kwesi Johnson, Black Uhuru, U-Roy, Culture, The Ethiopians, Israel Vibration, Tony Rebel and Garnett Silk and the list can go on.

My focus on "Blackness" was ubiquitous in my journey and my older brother's life. As I was evolving in greater consciousness of my African self, my expectations were greater, and I became more confident in my self-efficacy, voice and decision making.

This new way of being created some dissonance in our family as there was concern about how we would exist in a "White" world that did not adhere to and rejected these values. My mother embraced aspects of our journey as she recognized that there was a power in the voice that we were creating. The impact of our transformation influenced her thinking, values, and aesthetics. For my father, our way of existing in the world challenged him at his core. As someone who lived through the 50s and 60s during the pivotal years of the Civil Rights and Black Power Movements, he was aware of some of the schools of thought into which we were delving. He recognized the value of our study and the impact it had on our identity, yet he was deeply concerned about how we would function in a society that was intricately woven with the values, interests, and priorities that a "White male" dominated society established. At the root of his concern was how will we earn an income in a society that rejects an African worldview and perspective? How will we be able to navigate racism, discrimination, racial profiling, and the other by-products of White oppression? How would we be able to assimilate into this culture and "play the game" that would ensure that we could live a quality of life that provides a sense of security in this world?

Another major challenge was that many of the family traditions, norms, and practices that he embraced and valued were now being rejected. Our new African-centered enlightenment led me and my brother to abandon Christmas, Easter and other European holidays and customs. As we continued to grow in enlightenment and introduce culturally centered and relevant ways of living, the more my father felt isolated, awkward and like an outsider. It seemed like he did not know his place and value in the lives of his sons, and I am sure he never envisioned that he would feel disconnected and uneasy in the presence of his sons.

As we were all attempting to learn this unfamiliar dance and how to co-exist, our deep love for each other helped us to get through. We still gathered for family celebrations, yet the thrill of the occasion was slightly compromised. There were adjustments to the menu as we no longer ate meat. We now introduced Kwanzaa, which was embraced, yet it was different and from my father's perspective I am sure it felt weird at first. One thing about my father was he stayed connected to us. He opened himself up to the experiences that my brother and I exposed him to, not because they resonated with him; it was more to maintain the relationship and enter the domain of our influences. Over time my father began to value some of the new rituals and ceremonies as they created more intimacy and invited our family to a greater sense of belonging and connection. We also maintained some of the old ones that reflected our earlier passages and remained sacred to our connection. My father was a big sport enthusiast; he particularly had a love for track and boxing. These activities continued to be a mainstay in our lives as we gathered and conversed about track meets, boxing matches, Super Bowls, and NBA Finals. Though the sports interest was waning in my world, I always maintained enough interest to make sure that my father and I would be able to connect about the art and science of warriorship displayed through athletics.

On one sweltering day in the summer of 1989, I came home to what would be a devastating blow to my Spirit and a deeper entry into the liminal phase. Our family had recently moved from Greenburgh, NY to Marlton, NJ. My father accepted a transfer with his position at the Housing Urban Development (HUD) and relocated to Philadelphia. I did not yet feel the impact of the move as I was spending most of my time away at school in Hampton, VA. I was not thrilled to be in Marlton as I enjoyed returning home to my friends, family and the memories of my neighborhood and community. Most of my friends from my neighborhood that went away to college would return home and we would be able to connect, reflect on old times and be present to our new lives as young adults. Also, I was in my first meaningful relationship with a young woman who was from Greenburgh and lived in the Bronx. One of the benefits of living in Marlton was Philadelphia was not too far away and my brother was in graduate school at Temple University. In fact, that summer I spent most of my time in Philadelphia as I worked as a Residential Counselor at Temple University's Upward Bound Program. In Philadelphia, I was able to continue to feed my appetite for my Knowledge of Self quest as there was a strong and vibrant cultural community, arts scene, mosque, and Black bookstores.

One muggy day, Friday afternoon, I was returning to Marlton for the weekend. My girlfriend and I entered, and we placed our bags in one of the bedrooms. I heard someone in my parents' room and as I approached their room, I met my father at the entrance of his room. He greeted us and told me to come into the room. I told my girlfriend that I would be right back. As I entered the room, I noticed that there were clothes on the bed and luggage on the floor. My father's energy seemed prickly and tense. I asked him where he was going as his job required him to travel from time to time. He sighed and blurted out, "Things are not working out with me and your mother. I'll be moving out...not too far from here...Just up the road...." I was dumbfounded when I began to internalize what was being shared. I had no words. I just laid down at the bottom of the bed and wailed. My father continued to pack and let me know that he would be in communication with me to let me know where he was staying. I had no words. Once packed, he awkwardly and urgently departed. He said some words that were inaudible and exited. At that moment I entered the heart of the liminal. Our family and home would never be the same. Where would I consider home now? Who was I without my family unit? How would I navigate and negotiate the tension and friction between my parents? What could I do to support their healing process? What must I do to maintain the motivation to finish school? How would I establish a home for myself?

I never considered the Spiritual, psychological, and emotional safety that a home provides. For many years after my parents separated and later divorced, I felt empty and unstable. Though I was away at school, whenever I returned there was a feeling of rootlessness. Sure, I had places to rest my head, eat good meals and experience love from family members and friends; yet I yearned for the feelings of sanctity, comfort, and security of what became my idea of home. I remained in the liminal phase for an extended period wondering who were we as a family and who was I outside of the grounding of a home? The blessing in this trial is that for 19 years, I experienced the gift of home and the powerful medicine that comes from being loved, nurtured, challenged, and valued by a family living under one roof.

Once I completed school, it took me moving from three different locations before I even contemplated creating a sacred space for myself. One day my drum teacher came to visit and help me with maintenance on my drum. He began to ask for the tools needed. Do you have an awl? Screwdriver? Sandpaper? For every request, it took me 20 minutes to locate the items. He bluntly stated, "you need to stay home and get settled, brother." "Stop running all over...let people and life come to you." His charge helped me to realize that it was time for me to establish my own personal anchoring, comfort, and grounding. I realized that I needed support with transforming an apartment into a home. My mother, with her expert ability to create systems and her interior design gifts, played a significant role in helping me to establish a concept of a home that aligned with that phase of my young adult life. Once this occurred, I was able to stop running hastily all over the New York Metropolitan area in an unconscious search for a home.

Formalizing the Rites of Passage Trials

"In the present era, there exists a severe lack of essential rites of passage, a phenomenon often raised when examining the societal circumstances of today."

My personal reflections reveal trials that were presented by life events that were not formalized by *Jegnas* or community Elders. My experiences were occurrences that were a part of life's design and significant to my personal progression and elevation. The informal initiation birthed out of life's challenges can be powerful if you are aware of the gifts that an initiation can bring. The gift of wisdom, enlightenment, confidence, mastery of skills, the power of rituals, awareness of talents and how to use the talents to serve your Divine purpose are all available through the process of mastering the trials that come through the Rites of Passage process.

As a *Jegna*, one of your main responsibilities will be to create and choreograph trials that help to guide the initiate to the doorways of their dormant intelligence and uncultivated potential. Unlike the initiations that took place during ancient times, the modern day *Jegnas* must walk a delicate line to create all the provisions necessary to ensure the safety of the initiates (mentally, emotionally, Spiritually, and physically). The notion of safety when crossing uncharted thresholds seems oxymoronic. Indigenous people who still practice the initiation rites from an authentic expression of their heritage are not influenced by the modern standards of safety, as it is well known that an initiate will experience the lessons that pain and dissonance teach in the transformation process. The Indigenous practitioners of the initiation rites always recognized there was a possibility that the initiate would not only experience a metaphoric death; there was a chance that he or she might physically die. In the book, *Of Water and Spirit* by Malidoma Somé, he shares the dilemma that his village faced when he returned from being *taken from his Dagara village by a Jesuit priest and brought to a boarding school more than a hundred miles away. Here, the Jesuits were hoping to build a cadre of African missionaries to help convert the native population. Somé remained there for fifteen years of education, indoctrination, and various forms of physical and sexual abuse. He escaped at the age of nineteen and managed to find his way back to his village, where he was a stranger to his own people, unable to speak the language, uneducated in the ways of his ethnic group, and an object of suspicion because of his Western education and ability to read and write. In a final attempt to reintroduce him to village life, he was sent on a month-long initiation with a group of other village boys, most of them much younger than him.* The village elders assessed that he suffered from what they described as a terminal knowledge (the ability to read and write) and would not be able to endure the rigors of the Dagara initiation. According to Somé, "There are certain types of knowledge that deletes the opportunity of accessing other areas of knowledge." Some of the elders did not think that he would be able to survive the trials that were informed by the Spiritual intelligences and other worldly dimensions that are rooted in Dagara initiation and life. They thought that he would die physically if he participated in the initiation as he no longer had the Dagara Spiritual perception of life and would not be able to endure the rigorous supernatural trials he would encounter during his initiation.

Rite of Passage trials in the modern context must reinforce to the initiate that he is safe and that even though we are entering into unknown dimensions of their lives that will unquestionably create dissonance, pain and fear, there will be someone present with them to ensure that they are supported during the trials. Ritualizing the intent about maintaining safety (physically, mentally, emotionally, and physically) is extremely significant, yet it is equally important to acknowledge that the trials can show undesirable aspects, that the initiates' ego may be challenged and that there may be some moments that are unfamiliar to the initiate that may cause vulnerability, fear, trauma, uncertainty, doubt, and discomfort. Lastly, at the root of the trials choreographed in the rites of passage, two of the major concepts that inform the ordeals are confronting fear and enduring pain. All these "undesirable" mental, emotional, physical, and Spiritual states are significant *teachers* that deliver invaluable lessons during the initiation process. These "teachers" guide initiates to greater depths and higher states of enlightenment. They are the guides that help reveal the unexamined narratives that most are reluctant to face on their own and they help to awaken intelligences that are essential to knowing and mastering the self.

It is important that *Jegnas* are aware of their own formal and informal trials that reflects the isolating trauma and liminal phases of their transition from boyhood to adulthood, or any transition from one stage of life to another. The following are guided questions centered on the trials that you have experienced in your own journey. Answer these questions as honestly as possible as it is important to be aware of them as a *Jegna* charged with the responsibility of facilitating trials and holding space for the initiates who will be going through formalized experiences or processing the ordeals presented by life:

1. Describe a traumatic experience that occurred in your life. How has this event shaped how you currently view life?

2. Describe a time when you experienced a hardship and you felt like no one knew or would comprehend what you were going through. Or describe a time you were too embarrassed or ashamed to share what was occurring. How did you address this dilemma?

3. Describe a time where you felt overwhelmed by life trials and began to question your capacity to make good decisions or overcome the obstacles that you were experiencing. How did you navigate through this challenging time?

4. Describe a time when you felt like you did not know yourself anymore; a time when you exhausted the identity of who you once were and did not know your next plan of action in your becoming process. Reflect on a time when you felt stuck or stagnant. How did you navigate this season of life?

5. Describe a formal experience that you had where someone orchestrated, or you challenged yourself by engaging in activities/trials that were designed to cross thresholds or take you out of your comfort zone.

6. Describe a life experience where you were abruptly taken out of your routine and comfort zone and were thrust into events that challenged you to your core.

Trials for the Initiates

Now it is time to create trials for the initiates. Again, Rites of Passage trials help to prepare initiates for the mental, emotional, physical, and Spiritual ordeals that will inevitably be experienced in life. It would be beneficial to know about some of the challenges that have occurred in the initiates' life so that the trials can be an invitation to overcome the obstacles that might be blocking the gift and purpose that yearns to be awakened. As *Jegnas* you should be exploring the issues that would stifle the maturation process of the initiate. What are the barriers that prevent boys and young men of African and Indigenous Ancestry from being their true and best selves? The following questions/prompts are designed to help the initiates uncover the formal and informal trials that they have encountered and provide the content that will be used to create individual and collective trials.

1. Describe two major challenges that you experienced in your life. How did you overcome these challenges? What were the lessons that these challenges taught you? If someone were experiencing these challenges, what advice would you give them?

2. Describe a time when you were going through a challenging time, and you felt alone during the process. How did you attempt to resolve this experience? What was the outcome? What lessons were learned through this lonely period?

3. Describe a time in your life where you felt lost, confused, and did not have a clue on how you were going to deal with the situation. What lesson(s) were learned through this experience? How did you attempt to overcome this phase of your life?

The following are prompts that you will present to the initiates at various stages within their initiation. These questions for some may be trials within themselves, yet they can also be used to design trials. Role playing, simulations, illustrations, release rituals, affirmation rituals, journal writing, poetry/rap, musical entrainment exercises and mirror activities are just some of the methods that can be used to facilitate low inference and radical trials.

Musical Entrainment Exercises:
These are listening methods used to identify music that aligns with a person's emotions, mental states, and experiences they have gone through in their life. It is also used for envisioning where someone desires to be in life.

1. My life is like that of… (explain the similarities)
2. The way to success is…
3. My world would be perfect if…
4. I am different from most in my family and friends in that I…
5. My life would be drastically different if…
6. The person who has caused me the most pain is…
7. I am most happy when…
8. I am excited about my life because…
9. In 10 years, I will most likely be…

10. If I could change one thing about my life, I would change…

11. The strangest thing that ever happened to me was…

12. My purpose in life is…

13. My favorite childhood memory is when…

14. Sometimes I dream of…

15. My greatest fear is…

16. Since becoming a teen, I have gotten pretty good at…

17. I really admire… (name a person) because…

18. I am drawn to an animal. I always see this animal in real life or in my dreams. That animal is…

19. I belong to… (what ethnic group?) I know this because…

20. My thoughts about being a Black/Brown boy/young man is…

21. If this stage of my life were a song, the title would be…

22. If my life expression was a musical note, it would come from… (what instrument?)

23. I connect most with what natural element… (fire, water, air, earth, or mineral?) because…

24. When I become an Ancestor, I will be remembered for…

(Note: Questions #1-21 were crafted by high-ranking Rites of Passage *Jegna* and Warrior Baraka Moyo, Executive Director, PRIDE Rites of Passage and Akoben Enterprise Facilitator Trainer)

These questions/prompts do not have to be answered all at once. These inquiries can be presented as reflections, rituals, or essential questions during the sessions. The information gathered from these sessions will be helpful when designing trials for the initiates as they help to provide a barometer on the affirmative growth of the boys and young men, as well as some of the thresholds that are necessary to cross for their maturation, transformation, and manhood development.

The great task of the *Jegnas* will be to frame these questions and create trials informed by the Trauma/Isolation and Liminal phases of the initiation process.

Another significant area that *Jegnas* will have to consider when creating trials are what are the competencies necessary for healthy African and Indigenous manhood in the 21st century? What type of world will the initiates have to navigate in the next 25 years? What are the intelligences, sensibilities and attributes that will ensure that the initiates are able to make meaningful and purpose driven contributions to their families, community, people, and world?

For the *Jegnas* to begin creating trials centered on 21st century competencies, here are some themes that can be explored in collective discussions that will support the trial designing process:

1. What does the ideal family of African, Indigenous and Latino origins look like in the 21st century and beyond? What are the skills, values, commitments, and practices that men living in the 21st century must possess to ensure a healthy family dynamic?

2. What community values are essential for our boys and young men to possess as 21st century leaders and community members?

3. What values and skills are necessary for boys and young men entering adulthood in the 21st century to possess in their careers and vocations?

4. What are the local, national, and international issues that are impeding the progress of people of African, Indigenous and Latino Ancestry? What values, skills and knowledge will be necessary to prepare the boys and young men to successfully address these issues? How will our people's lives be different once these issues are resolved?

5. What does optimal health (Spiritual, Mental, Emotional and Physical) look like in our communities?

6. What legacy will be realized when our boys' become men and begin to execute the Divine design of their lives?

As *Jegnas*, you are assigned to co-create these meaningful discussions with members of your community (elders, *Jegnas*, *Djelis*—the keepers of our collective stories and customs, artists, parents, community members and initiates) to establish clear objectives that will serve as the guides and pillars to the manhood development process. Through intentional discussions, the aim is to create a core minimum value system, concepts and experiences that reflect the best of what our community envisions as optimal manhood for the 21st century and beyond. The design of these trial frameworks should not come from one member or one group. Representatives from the diverse members within our community (African, Indigenous, Latinx) should be invited to the discussion for the purpose of offering their perspectives on the ideals of manhood, the essential needs of our communities and the roles and responsibilities that we see men serving to establish a safe and healthy culture and climate in our communities.

Young men from UAAHC (Bronx, NY) presenting a step performance (Trial)
4th Annual Coalition of Schools Educating Boys of Color Gathering
of Leaders Young Men's Passage
Howard University, Washington, DC, 2010

Below are themes for which trials can be created:

- Leadership capacity
- Presentation of core values
- Confronting fears/demonstrating courage.
- Facilitation of rituals
- Oral communication skills
- Emotional intelligence
- Social skills
- Martial art techniques/military strategy
- Pain management (emotional, physical)
- Physical tests
- Critical thinking and centered decision making
- Creative thinking and improvisational skills
- Healthy relationships
- Identifying, claiming, and living with purpose
- Constructive behavior
- Confronting the "slave and colonized mentality"
- All competencies significant to being a young man in the 21st century (Know Thyself – our story and culture), career mapping, financial literacy, health and wellness plans, branding, internal and external martial arts, male-female relationships, chakra awareness, etc.)
- What are the 21st century competencies that men of African, Indigenous and Latino Ancestry need to thrive in the modern world?(Refer to the above themes)
- How can we contextualize and create safe trials that will emote trauma and isolation? (Examples of modern-day trials that emote trauma/isolation; reflect on informal and formal)

✺ How can we create activities and exercises that guide the initiate to a state of liminality (the transition from the identity of the boy/young man prior to the initiation and the uncertain phase experienced before he earns his new title and status in the community)?

As a *Jegna*, it is important that you are cognizant of the multiple opportunities to contextualize any life endeavor (no matter how lofty or ordinary) as a trial. The intensive sacred trials of a rites of passage differ from some of the day-to-day experiences that occur in the mundane and profane expressions of life. However, as Jegnas, your ability to contextualize trials will provide a different level of intentionality that is sometimes missing when a call and response ritual is absent. The framing of trials is necessary so that there is a present awareness of whatever the initiate is called to engage or confront. When making the call to a trial, be sure to communicate the relevance of the trial as it connects to being a significant life skill and/or attribute of manhood. Share personal narratives about how the mastery of the trial has been significant in your life or to others in your sphere of influence and obligation. With the right framing, any challenge or assignment can be connected to something greater than a task that can be interpreted as just doing for the sake of doing. When creating trials be sure to not only make it relevant, also make sure that once completed that there are authentic opportunities for the skill, values, intelligences, and sensibilities to be integrated in a manner that has significance to the initiate, his family, and the community in which he resides. If the trial does not connect with something that matters to the initiate, it might be useful, yet not meaningful to him. As *Jegnas* we seek to be inspirers as opposed to manipulators. Whenever possible, be mindful of trials that you know speak to the initiate's passion, emerging purpose, and unique attributes. By doing so, you will not receive as much resistance to the trial and will serve as a bridge to the call that echoes within the initiate. Be sure to take notice of the initiate's qualities, interests, wounds, fears, and memories. It is this awareness that serves as fuel to designing personalized and collective trials.

Lastly, it will be of great significance to be aware of the anxiety and trauma that may surface as a trigger during certain trials. This is why it is significant for the *Jegnas* to experience the trials themselves so that they will have a frame of reference to comprehending what can potentially show up as a challenge or crisis for the initiate and be strategic about how to address the response to the ordeals.

Below are a few example trials that are centered on radical transformation on Spiritual, mental, and emotional levels, while others are geared towards personal life skills that build competencies that support the journey to manhood.

Vision Quest: A North American Indigenous ritual where an initiate leaves everything behind (childhood, home, material possessions) in search of personal communication and messaging from the Spirit world to receive a vision, insights or a sacred meaning that are induced by fasting, invocations, and other sacred practices during a time of prolonged isolation: typically undertaken by an adolescent male (See Appendix 1 for Facilitation Guide).

Seat of Ma'at: Ma'at is a sacred system of ethics that has its origins in the Nile Valley Civilizations of antiquity. It represents the moral ideal that citizens of Kemet (known today as Egypt) and other nation states of the Nile Valley strove to uphold as individuals and a society. The virtues of Ma'at are Truth, Justice, Propriety, Reciprocity, Balance, Order and Righteousness. Ma'at is always represented with an ostrich feather. In ancient Kemite cosmogony/theogeny it was believed that when a person dies their heart is weighed against the feather of Ma'at to access the goodness of their life. This weighing on the scales of justice was a ritual for determining if a newly deceased person would be permitted to enter the Afterlife. Only those individuals whose hearts were lighter than Ma'at's feather were permitted to pass through into immortality with the Divine. The heart that is burdened with the weight of guilt, shame, regret, anger, fear, greed, etc. would be sent to return to life and work through issues of the heart. The Kemetyu (as they called themselves) operated from the notion that intrinsically all people were potentially good.

Reflecting on these ancient virtues, the Spirit gifted me with a ritual called the Seat of Ma'at. The Seat of Ma'at process was presented as a trial for those who were courageous to investigate matters of the heart and explore the content of their minds. It provides an excellent value to the initiate who is at the crossroads of his life and in need to examine his core truths, value systems and current life circumstances that are impeding him from actualizing his life's purpose, calling, and goals. This process is also used when an individual is about to enter a new phase of their life and needs to rid the self of old attitudes, toxic emotions, and undesirable behaviors that they no longer want to carry with them in their next chapter of life. This symbolic death will "lighten the load" that guilt, fear, anger, or any other painful and traumatic experience may have on stunting the growth of one's Spiritual, mental, emotional, and moral progress. The ultimate intention for the Seat of Ma'at is to directly confront one's own thinking, explore patterns of behavior, identify strengths, acknowledge challenges, seek guidance, request assistance, embrace vulnerability as a gateway to enlightenment, and set a plan of action for transformation.

Members of a loving community serve as guides prepared to listen attentively, ask critical and clarifying questions, affirm identity, challenge thought and behavioral patterns and sympathetically charge their peers with some action steps that will help them move in a direction that align with their mission, goals, values, and core truths (See Appendix 2 for Facilitation Guide).

Eye of Heru: Heru is an ancient Kemetic Divine force of nature represented as a falcon's eye. Falcons are known for their keen sight, speed, and their ability to fly high in the sky. Also, Falcons can look directly into the sun without harming their eyes. The Eye of Heru represents awareness and protection from negativity.

The Eye of Heru ritual involves making direct eye contact with a brother, while reflecting on questions centered on identity, purpose, vulnerabilities, and infinite possibilities. The trial strengthens intuitive sensibilities, communication, self-worth, and vision. Additionally, the Eye of Heru builds brotherhood bonds and invites initiates to use their intuitive intelligences to convey Spirit inspired messages.

Additionally, this ritual intentionally supports with activating and encouraging the spirit of *Sawubona*, the South African Zulu greeting that translates to "I see you" in English. The acknowledgement of being seen is an invitation to embrace community bonds and intimacy which establishes a powerful kinship, belonging and connectivity. The Eye of Heru ritual helps our community confront the anxiety that emerges when making eye contact and being "seen" by others in a way that penetrates the social masks that we wear. I have witnessed on numerous occasions confrontations (sometimes leading to violence) beginning from a simple look or a stare. (See Appendix 3 for Facilitation Guide)

Promise Land Trial: The Promised Land is a Biblical reference where Abraham agreed that he and his descendants would obey and worship God and lead by example. Hebrews believed that God and Abraham entered a covenant in which God promised many descendants, a blessed nation, and a Promised Land.

In the quest for freedom, people of African Ancestry used this "Promise Land" passage and Gospel Hymn reference to interpret our collective plight as people who were in bondage under the cruel system of slavery. The "Promised Land "in the enslaved African imagination, lived up to being an egalitarian utopia for fugitives in many ways. In Canada, slavery was denounced in 1793 and was formally abolished in 1834. Many enslaved Africans put their lives on the line and escaped the plantation to journey north in quest for freedom, if necessary, even to Canada.

The Promised Land Trial takes place in a remote forest area where the initiates experience a simulated Underground Railroad route to freedom. At each Underground Railroad station, the initiates are asked questions by *Jegnas* about information that they should have mastered during their initiation. If answered correctly, the Guides of the Underground Railroad share clues on how to get to the next Underground Railroad station. The initiates must be watchful of the simulated slave catchers that search the trails for runaways (See Appendix 4 for Facilitation Guide).

Elemental Immersion Initiation:

Inspired by Dagara Indigenous Spiritual Technology, initiates experience sacred rituals designed to release, restore, reconnect, and affirm a purpose-driven life. Through Earth, Fire, Water, and Mineral rituals, this Elemental Immersion initiation guides aspirants to the infinite wisdom of the elemental teachers who support us in the remembrance of our gifts and purpose and help to clear internal impediments that block us from actualizing the Divine assignment that we are here to express (See Appendix 5 for Facilitation Guide).

Physical Trials:

Though the primary focus of these trials is to test physical strength and stamina, mental, emotional, and Spiritual aptitudes are equally significant when competing or training. The physical trials are incorporated in the initiates rituals, routines, and daily norms. Initially, all initiates will be tested in basic calisthenics. Once a baseline assessment is made, it is the responsibility of the initiate to exceed the performance of his last trial (if an initiate maxed at 40 push-ups, he will have to do more the following month). The initiate is charged to cross the physical thresholds and challenge himself to confront fear and endure the pain that comes from pushing past limits. The young men will hear and become aware of their internal voice that either inspires or discourages them to perform at their maximum level. Throughout the passage, the initiates will learn how to use their mental and emotional intelligences to transcend the discomfort that their physical will endure during the trials.

Budgeting Trials:

Financial literacy and money management are necessary competencies for 21st century manhood. Comprehending financial systems and how to build financial wholeness are critical concepts and practices for our community. Having initiates reflect on their values and how they engage with money will be a key foundational step in establishing healthy financial practices that support their goals, principles, and unfolding purpose. Learning the tenets and practices of financial planning will be essential for initiates to master money as a tool to help manifest their visions in a methodical and responsible manner.

Independent Traveling:

As initiates begin to seek independence and desire to venture farther away from home, *Jegnas* will establish trials to test their capacity to successfully navigate walking directions and public transportation. Having the initiates plan a trip and present their route will support them in their quest. In the age of Google and GPS, the initiates will have tools to reach their destination. For safety measures, the *Jegnas* can check in with the initiates via text, shadow them from a distance and meet them at the agreed upon end point.

The Beauty, Honor, Sacredness and Powers of Girls and Women:

Gaining awareness of the sacred Divine feminine and masculine expressions of life is essential to creating harmony, balance, and order to the complementary nature of women and men. As male-dominated patriarchal systems have governed the planet through millenniums, it is necessary to challenge our notion of the roles established by our society and reimagine relationships centered on the complementary nature of the Divine feminine and masculine and how we can establish relationships that honor and support these principles as they both live within males and females. Initiates will learn the qualities of these principles and how they both live within them, as well as how to best cultivate these principles with each other and the girls and women that are in their sphere of influence and obligation.

Declaration and Oath Statement:

As initiates master trials, overcome obstacles and cross major thresholds, it will be necessary to memorialize their major passages. One of their final trials will be to create and make a public declaration of their intentions and commitments to themselves and the community. The Oath Statement will serve as their re-integration to the community after the formal passage is over. It lets the village know the initiate's purpose and what we can expect from him as he embarks on his next chapter in life. It is publicly expressed so that the community can hold the initiate accountable to the path that he has chosen for himself. It also serves as a reminder and guide for him to refer to when life challenges make him weary, confused, and doubtful.

The following are a few other trials that *Jegnas* can assign to initiates:

- Cook Meals for the Family
- Perform Rituals
- Create and Present a Vision Board
- Community Service
- Shop for the Household
- Read Instructions and Assemble Furniture
- Create and Present the Family Tree
- Significant Lessons from Our Story—Frame Our People's Narrative
- Read and Comprehend Food Labels
- Recite Sacred Text and Create Affirmations
- Create Personal, Family and Community Rituals
- Wash and Iron Clothes
- Self-Defense Trials
- Engaging Law Enforcement
- Check the Oil and Tires on the Family Car
- Plan a Weekly Schedule of Activities
- Create a Balanced Wardrobe for All Occasions
- Clean the Bathroom Completely
- Set the Table for a Formal Family Dinner/Event

- Paint an Entire Room at Home
- Maintain Plants or a Small Garden
- Name Local Leaders (Formal and Informal)
- Learn About Currency and Financial Systems
- Pack a Car Trunk for Family Trip
- Change a Light Bulb
- Find Independent Educational Opportunities that Align with Interests and Mission
- Learn and Perform CPR
- Establish Good Nutritional Practices
- Create and Schedule Monthly Appointments
- Consistently Check on a Senior Citizen
- Ask Intelligent Questions in Public
- Write a Business Proposal
- Create Presentations or PowerPoint
- Cultivate V.O.I.C.E (Victory Over Insecurities Causes Elevation)
- Learn a New Language

It is important for *Jegnas* to be deliberate about establishing a sacred intention and contextualizing the experiences with why it is significant and the benefits that will be gained once the initiate masters the knowledge, skills, and values that the trial will challenge. Additionally, *Jegnas* should invite community members who have a specialization and mastery of the discipline that is being tested. This makes the trial authentic and creates an ambience of integrity. The goal is for the initiate to approach the challenge knowing that the task will be serious, and that they will be held to a high standard. Each trial should yield some level of the unexpected so that the initiate will have to confront their trepidations and be present to the moment.

CHAPTER FOUR

ENLIGHTENMENT

"Transformation mirrors the rebirth of a phoenix from its own ashes. From the fiery end emerges a renewed, regal creature, symbolizing profound and enduring change."

—*Kamau Ptah*

Following the Rites of Passage sequence, enlightenment comes from the lessons of the trauma/isolation and liminal phases. There is a wisdom that comes from turning down the voice of the ego, experiencing extreme discomfort, enduring pain, and confronting fear. The initiate gains profound insights and degrees from dissonant teachers. The dark taboos and shadows of life give birth to enlightenment. Once an initiate liberates himself from the attachment to the wounds and the relationship with the narrative that justifies his condition, he can value the trials that helped to produce the wisdom and powers that are earned by enduring the arduous challenges experienced through the initiation process. The trials gift him with a medicine that becomes his superpower and cultivates his distinctive Spiritual signature. The passage leads the initiate to his inner pathway of transcendence. John Bolling articulates this phenomenon as the act of "going beyond" one stage of growth to the next higher stage of growth. Transcendence is an act of going beyond what sometimes seems like insurmountable barriers and impossible problems in development to find a peaceful, creative, and growth-oriented solution. The ability to go within and come back out with a renewed energy to go beyond is unique to the transcendent spiritual element of the African and Indigenous Soul-centered worldview and ancient technologies that derive from these cultures. This distinct transcendental quality of Spirit which W.E.B. DuBois described as "The Gift of Black Folk" allows aspirants to develop through initiation, reflection and dialogue, a new sense of altruistic duty (duty for the common good of the family, extended family, community, people, ethnic/national group, Mother Nature, or the Cosmos). This new sense of duty would include a sense of responsibility, commitment and right action directed not towards the selfish self but towards the collective community, the group self or Soul (Bolling, p. 139).

As the trial lessons guide the initiate to the threshold of his new call, it is still the choice of the initiate to accept the gifts, powers, and insights that have been bestowed upon him. It is the initiate that now births himself through the "contraction field" and he must decide whether he accepts the responsibilities of his newfound enlightenment and his call. If the call is accepted, the initiate steps out of the threshold world as a newborn, yet this time he is not innocent, naked, or helpless. This time he is walking tall and carrying himself with balance and purpose. The essential question that must be answered is, "For what purpose am I entering this new world?" There will still be some uncertainty as to how to execute this purpose and that is perfectly fine. Much of the wisdom and gifts of the trials unfold after the initiate returns. A seed has been sown in the initiate: a knowing about himself that cannot be forgotten.

UAAHC scholar, Brother Elias Encarnacion, affectionately known
as Brother Red, shares his enlightenment on a panel discussion
10th Annual COSEBOC Gathering of Leaders Youth Passages
Jacob Javits Center, New York City, 2016.
Credit for photograph – Jamaica Jackson, Jamaica Jackson Photography.

The Elemental Immersion Initiation

Amid the Global Initiation that was spawned by the coronavirus, I
heard the call to participate in Malidoma Somé's Elemental Immersion Initiation. I call this period a Global Initiation as it mirrors the
dynamics of a rites of passage experience. During this time many had to
confront themselves and journey through trials as the shutdown forced
us to slow down and focus on what is most essential to our lives. To
intensify this initiation, I was also unexpectedly terminated from my
job as a Director for the Gaining Awareness and Readiness for Undergraduate Programs (GEAR UP). Now that my day-to-day routines and
norms were disrupted, I had to really focus on the question, "Who am
I?" from the core of my identity. I began to reflect on the areas of my
life that are often neglected and pondered about who I am Spiritually,
mentally, emotionally, and physically. I began to deepen my exploration

of the meaning of my life and became very intentional about examining my Divine assignment at this unique time of history. What is my greatest value to myself, my family, my community, the planet, and the universe? What really matters to me? How can I use my gifts and purpose to contribute to the elevation and growth of my family, community, my people, and the world?

I started to be intentional about my ritual practices. When I awakened every dawning, I would start my day with meditation, exercise, journaling, and our family ritual. Once the intentions for my day were established, I would begin to show up to what I determined to be the most authentic call to my mission. In the past, my ritual was modified as I would have to rush off to work to beat the morning traffic. I now had the opportunity to show up to my call without what I considered to be an impediment to my Divine purpose, which was my job. In all my work experiences there were aspects of my mission that were able to be expressed, yet it always felt like I was eating without tasting. As an educator devoted to liberating the hearts and minds of children of African and Indigenous Ancestry, I would constantly struggle to find ways to execute cultural frameworks, methods, and practices behind enemy lines (public school *miseducation* systems). It is/was two opposing philosophies and systems sprinting in different directions. My mission created a lot of dissonance and opposition to the culture and climate that public schools have established to maintain and sustain the status quo. Though my termination was abrupt, I saw this as a Divine intervention to deepen my work as a rite of passage and healing-centered engaged practitioner. Once I worked on aligning my Spiritual beingness through rituals, I began to attract experiences and resources that enabled me to engage directly with what I consciously know as my Divine purpose.

The highest priorities for me were to begin to work on this book, which was long overdue. Since 2003, I have entertained the notion of taking my graduate school thesis on rites of passage and translating it into a book. There were several attempts, yet the internal blockages and habit of placing other things of importance over my book, prevented me from building consistency. As time lapsed, I would tell myself that the information that I started this process with was outdated and irrelevant to the changes that were happening in the community, and my expanded knowledge of rites needed a new and fresh interpretation from what I was offering in 2003. Additionally, my traveling and work of helping communities establish rites of passage were occupying a great deal of time and I did not feel like I was able to center myself to write. Now that I did not have "work" responsibilities, I was able to show up with a greater focus and laser sharp attention to what I know to be a significant aspect of sharing my mission as a rites of passage leader and practitioner.

I also began to respond to the call of personal initiations to help me to cultivate the dormant intelligences within that are centered on being an instrument for healing. I have never viewed my assignment as a work of healing, yet I have witnessed wherever I have administered rites of passage that those who have been engaged in the initiation process have transformed their lives from the core and were able to go through a radical transformation/healing. In fact, not only were the young men impacted by these initiations, their families and communities were significantly affected.

I have been intrigued by Malidoma Somé's work since the early nineties. I was first introduced to his narrative as a Junior High School teacher in Harlem. I had a student in my class who was enlightened beyond his years on the path to "Know Thyself." It was clear that his parents raised and immersed him in African- centered culture and practices throughout his young life. He represented the counter-narrative to most children of African and Indigenous Ancestry who were miseducated about their historical and cultural legacy in the New York City Public School System. He thought, walked, and communicated with a confidence that was distinct and it was clear that his rearing was intentional. As a student, he valued my mission as a teacher who was devoted to ensuring that students were deeply exposed and engaged to their historical and cultural narratives. One day after an engaging lesson, he approached me, handed me a book, and said, "I think you would really enjoy this book. I was given this book as a gift through my rites of passage program (He was an initiate in the Blue Nile Rites of Passage Program in Harlem's Abyssinia Church). The book was *Of Water and Spirit* by Malidoma Patrice Somé. I was familiar with Somé as I had a few cassettes of his talks at the First World Alliance and the United African Movement, both notable grassroots organizations that hosted prominent scholars, leaders, activists, cultural custodians, and Spiritual practitioners. I was blown away that one of my students would offer me a book that was authored by one of the emerging deep thinkers of that era, who was revealing the profound wisdom teachings, healing, and Spiritual practices of his Dagara village.

As I read the book, I was amazed by the ritual practices, initiations, customs, traditions, ceremonies, and magic of the Dagara people. As I learned about these sophisticated socialization systems and healing practices, I felt deprived, angered, and envious that I did not grow up in a culture where life affirming and sustaining systems existed. I was aware of how enslavement and colonialization severed those from the African Diaspora from our Indigenous intelligences and sensibilities. Yet, *Of Water and Spirit* clearly exhibited the methods that were used to cultivate the faculties of what it means to be a healthy Spirit that resides in the flesh. My spirit yearned to experience an initiatory rite that would contribute to my identity formation, clarity of my purpose and how to use my gifts to deliver my purpose. I have intuitively known that these types of rites are significant to the full maturation and greatest expression of one's purpose and gifts. Though it would be years later before I met Malidoma Somé, it was learning about his narrative that opened my mind to the greater expression of initiatory work.

Darnell and I loaded up the car and were excited to go on an adventure together to Asheville, North Carolina to experience The Gathering of Men - 4 Day Ritual Intensive facilitated by Elder Malidoma. Darnell and I met in 1987 when I first arrived at Hampton University (HU). We immediately connected as we were both on our paths to cultivate and hone our voices as men and leaders committed to establishing a sacred space for our peers to identify, claim and live their purpose through reconnecting with their historical and cultural identity. Like many who came before us, we assumed that we would receive an educational experience that was centered on addressing the identity crisis and inter-generational trauma that we suffered as a people for the past four hundred plus years. Many believed that the Historically Black College and University (HBCU) journey at Hampton would be designed to repair the deep-rooted oppressive conditions in communities of African and Indigenous Ancestry. We were sorely mistaken once we discovered that the miseducation enterprise was very much operative at Hampton. The curriculum and practices were still rooted in white supremacist racism, yet they were executed in "Black Face" sometimes with the "Black" cultural style. Darnell, myself, and a few other students were charged by the Ancestors with creating a sacred space for students who were on a quest to enlightenment through the "Knowledge of Self" path. We pioneered what would be known as the African Studies Cluster. This was the genesis of my brotherhood with Darnell Smith.

As we embarked on our 15-hour quest, we reflected a great deal on our lives and how far we have journeyed since Hampton University. We both acknowledged that at the core of our missions, from the time we met until the present, we were fueled by healing intentions. It was only looking through the rearview mirror of life that we were able to see the uniting thread and make connections to having a deep desire for helping our community restore identity, community and purpose through customs, rituals, and indigenous ways of thinking, knowing and being. Now we were in route to participate in an experience that would jump start the next venture of our lives. We had no idea what was in store for us. As we continued to ruminate about our lives, I recall Darnell jokingly suggesting that "we about to go down here and they gonna bury our asses." We both laughed as he was referencing what we read in Malidoma's book about one of his initiatory trials of being buried alive. After the laughter waned, there was a silent pause and a short glance. I asserted, if that is one of the activities, I am ready. We had no idea what we were entering into when we responded to the next level of our manhood and leadership call.

The introductory question that Malidoma initiated the group engagement with was, "What horse did you ride into town on?" Many of the men were initially confused and needed greater clarification. Malidoma explained, "we all have narratives that have crafted our decision to travel here for the five-day intensive. Share the call that you heard and what prompted you to follow the call. Many men spoke about the grief and wound narratives that translated to a need to rid themselves of the societal masks they had been wearing. After hearing everyone's sharing, it appeared that most men in attendance had exhausted their strategies for living a fulfilled and purpose-driven life and needed an experience that would cultivate a new way of viewing themselves and reconnect with their interior world to re-imagine a life that was aligned with the assignment they agreed to accomplish on the earth plane. Once everyone shared their testimonies, Malidoma looked to one of his facilitators with a furtive smile and asked, "What do you think?" The middle-aged man responded, "It sounds like earth to me." What he was referring to was performing what is known by the Dagara people as a Radical Earth Ritual or Earth Immersion Initiation. The Elemental Immersion Initiations are designed to restore our relationship with the visible worlds of nature and community and one's relationship with the invisible forces of the Ancestors and Spirit Allies. According to the Dagara, Malidoma says, "The purpose of the earth ritual is to provide a sense of belonging, a remembrance of home, and an experience of being 'grounded' in the most literal sense." He further explains, "Earth is where we belong. She is our home. She gives us sustenance unconditionally and makes it possible for us to feel connected. Earth is where we go to and where we come from. The nourishment and support of the Earth grant us the feeling of belonging that allows us to expand and grow because we feel strong" (Somé Malidoma.com).

I looked at Darnell and we smiled with that look that conveyed, "It's about to go down." And yes, it was about to go down for real. In preparation for the Earth Ritual, we created groups and were instructed to dig our holes that would be able to hold the body of the largest person in the group. Darnell and I were partnered and began the pre-ritual process of digging our hole and placing our intentions with every poke into mother earth. Once we dug our hole, we made offerings to the earth and conveyed our intentions, aspirations and the challenges that obstructed our paths. Once the preparation ritual was completed, we waited for the sun to go down as these rituals are designed to occur when night falls.

It was a frigid Spring night in the mountains of Asheville, North Carolina. I was dressed in sweatpants and a hoody. None of what I was wearing mattered as the trial of the Earth Element ritual is to enter the earth naked! It is not a requirement, yet to maximize the experience and to receive all the earth's medicine, it was suggested to engage this test as our indigenous Ancestors had done for thousands of years. I took on the charge with a great deal of urgency. I prioritized this experience to fully invest in myself and was committed to operate with integrity and authenticity. I told myself, I have left my family and my daily routines and norms to respond to a call that lived in my bone and blood memory. I knew that this experience would create a demarcation in my life and set me on a path to live from the most genuine expression of myself. As I unclothed myself, I could feel the brisk air engulf my body. I entered the hole first and rested on the hard red earth. The men in my group began to place the dirt on top of me. As the cold earth began to cover my body, I felt held and comforted by mother earth. There were periods where I felt the earth's pulsation all over my body and I experienced heat, and it would be immediately and boldly interrupted by bone chilling cold. I focused on my breath as my mind vacillated from "why the hell are you doing this, to what was that rush that entered my body?" During the cold spells, where I experienced the chattering of my teeth and bones that felt like they were freezing, I discovered wisdom that can only emerge from subjecting yourself to this type of discord. I realized that there is intelligence in our bones and every time I trembled, I was able to breathe deeply, confront an undesirable area of my life and release the attachment to the thought, memory, and emotion. It was like Mother Earth conveyed messages that rattled and activated intelligences in my bones. It became clear to me that every time I quivered, it offered an opportunity for me to purge and surrender my wounds to Mother Earth. There was a rhythm that I became aware of that I interpreted as the contraction process that mothers experience during the birthing process, minus the excruciating labor pain that I could never imagine. Once I released the pain, I would feel the relief and strong hugging embrace of Mother Earth. There was a breathing pattern that I received from the Earth that supported this release and restoration procedure. This process continued for an hour and when my Spirt confirmed that I was complete, I requested to be dug out of the hole. Upon rising from the hole, I was assisted up and given some blankets to warm my body. We were then escorted to the fire pit where we were thawed out by the warmth of the fire's heat and gazed into the roaring of its medicine as we drank tea and silently contemplated the experience.

This radical ritual and immersion into Mother Earth provided a profound change in basic assumptions and enlightened me about the wisdom that emerges through the dark, shadowy, and cold dimensions of life. She introduced me to the medicine that she provides through ritual engagement and how to access my medicine with her guidance. She revealed to me the elements of earth that dwell within me and have gifted me with the tools to hold, nurture and support in the realignment and centering of my life and those who I am privileged to hold space for during their season of transformation. Lastly, I was made aware of the enormous magnitude of the earth's presence and her unconditional Love for humans, as well as the other natural elements and all that She yields in the act of creation. I recognized that I have those same qualities and can access them through radical rituals and daily maintenance rituals that invoke Her Spirit.

In addition to designing powerful trials for initiates, another significant role of a *Jegna* is to acknowledge when enlightenment occurs for the initiate. As *Jegnas* it is important to identify these moments, as sometimes the initiates will not have language to describe their newfound intelligence, consciousness, and sensibilities. Thoughts and language are inadequate to capture when the Spirit or mind has been transformed. The initiate will have a new energy and it may take some time to ground and integrate these powers into their lives. The *Jegna's* role is to help them find language, symbols and narratives that support them with recognizing their new awareness and the gifts that have now emerged.

As *Jegnas* reflect on the trials, daily life occurrences and threshold moments of their lives and the paths of the initiates, they should be present and observant of the following phenomena:

- "Aha" moments (recognition of moments where Spirit illuminates, the mental "lightbulb" shines and realization unfolds)

- Attitudinal shifts

- Awareness and deep reflection on thought and emotional patterns

- Recognition of wounds as lessons, as opposed to hard wired attachments and confusion of pain memories as "the self."

- The ability to know and articulate areas of vulnerability.

- The ability to craft and articulate questions to resolve life's challenges.

- Clarity on the lessons that pain, fear, and dissonance have taught and why it was essential for the initiate/student to experience these ordeals.

- The ability to step out of his comfort zones.

- The ability for the initiate to articulate his newfound sense of purpose and evolving gifts.

- The ability to be able to take concepts related to his purpose and gifts and make conscientious daily life decisions rooted in his developing mission and calling.

- The ability to integrate new skills, values, concepts, practices, qualities, and powers into their lives.

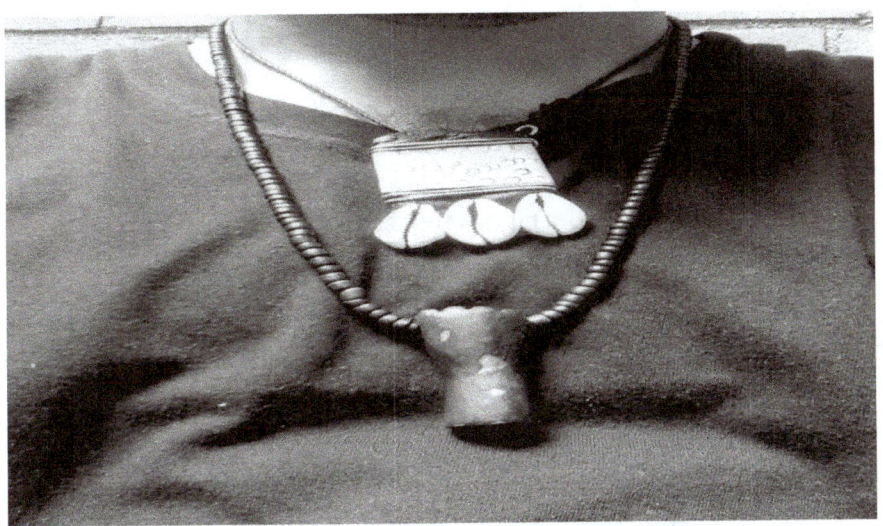

UAAHC scholar wears his necklaces earned for exhibiting
the core principles and possessing the character of an enlightened
UAAHC Warrior. UAAHC Bronx, NY, 2011

Reflective Questions on Enlightenment for *Jegnas*:

Describe at least two enlightening events that have occurred in your life. How did you arrive to enlightenment? What did the enlightening experiences teach you? How can others learn from what you experienced? How can you create trials and passages for the initiates to receive the gifts that you gained from your enlightened process?

Who were you prior to your enlightenment process? What were the greatest internal barriers that impeded your process? How were you able to navigate through the mental, emotional, physical, and spiritual obstacles? Who held space for you as you were experiencing breakthrough moments?

Why was it important for you to experience what you learned during your enlightenment process? How does this enlightenment serve your purpose today?

What rituals must be done to maintain and grow in your enlightened state?

What new privileges and responsibilities came along with attaining enlightenment?

What are some of the taboos that can sabotage and deter you from staying on your path to enlightenment?

Framing the Enlightenment for Initiates

It is of extreme significance for the *Jegnas* to facilitate deep reflection upon the completion of trials. There is no way of determining when enlightenment happens as it occurs at various times and is unpredictable. The initiate must be in a deep place of vulnerability, full presence, and acceptance of the teachers (lessons, experience, and people) that appear as trials in the rites of passage process. Wherever the trial takes the initiate, it is important that the *Jegna* is keenly attuned to what occurred and be prepared to process with the initiate. The collective voice of the *Jegnas* is significant as each *Jegna's* trained eye will see and assess the initiate's trial and shift from his unique perspective. Where appropriate, the initiates should also provide their points of view about how their peers completed the trial, or any paradigm shifts that were observed.

Again, the enlightenment phase highlights subtle and overt breakthroughs and transformations. Awakening arises through self-examination and the metaphors of nature. It might be challenging for the initiates to articulate in words this new consciousness, yet it can be captured in their body language and the stable presence of their energy. During this shift, initiates begin to see themselves as capable, competent, worthy, and powerful. Through confronting fears and navigating through pain, a new life emerges. Knowledge is gained. Confidence takes root. The young men begin to experience their capacity to thrive (*Rite of Passage* Open Sky (openskywilderness.com).

Based on the nature of the ritual trials and the *Jegna's* verbal acknowledgement of the initiates, it is encouraging to gift the initiate with something symbolic to recognize the mastery of the trial. The symbol should be relevant to the overarching call, as well as the nature of the trial. For example, I recall when I played Pop Warner Football, whenever someone sacked the quarterback, retrieved a fumble, or made an interception, he received a crossbones sticker. As a school administrator of an all-boys school that had rites of passage as a part of our mission and core practices, when I observed our scholars making self-determined decisions aligned with our core principles, I would invite them to my office along with members of the community that were a part of their circle of Love, influence and obligation and gift them with cultural necklaces or bracelets. These were what we called Warrior Acknowledgements. The necklace was a clinched fist, signifying power, and self-determination and the bracelet was interwoven with brass, silver, and copper. We referred to the bracelet as an *Ujima* Warrior (Collective Work and Responsibility) bracelet. The bracelets were gifted to the scholars who exhibited the concept of "wanting for my brother, what I want for myself." Noble acts of de-escalating conflicts, holding space for someone as they were going through a major challenge, being the voice for the voiceless, or mediating conflicts were behaviors that earned the acknowledgement of an Ujima UAAHC Warrior.

As you present the initiate with the gift, be sure to set the context that earned him the recognition. Describe to him and the gathered group that his behavior showed affirmative qualities that reflect the ideals that we are aspiring to live by in our learning community. Make sure you have each person share affirmative and uplifting remarks and offer encouragement to ensure that the initiate recognizes the value that he brings to the community.

The journey to enlightenment can be grueling in both the formal and informal initiation process. *Jegnas* must be present to hold space during the tough trials, particularly when the old identity deteriorates. Ego death can be excruciating, and the initiates will need someone that gives them permission to metaphorically die to old thought patterns, emotional attachments, pain memories and Spiritual blockages. In fact, the *Jegnas* will also need to strengthen their brotherhoods to support the lifelong cycles of constant transition, elevation, growth, and evolution. The dissonance and the discomfort that is felt helps to yield enlightenment. The road to enlightenment is a cycle of births, metaphoric deaths, and rebirths.

Setting the Context of Enlightenment for Initiates

As *Jegnas* you will have the task of setting the context for the initiates to experience all the rites of passage phases. The following are questions to support initiates with being reflective of the enlightening experiences that have occurred in their lives:

- Identify the people in your life that you feel really see and get to experience the true you. What do they see in you?

- Identify moments when someone shared a positive view of you that you were not aware that you possessed.

- Describe a time when you struggled with a challenge and had a breakthrough that gave you awareness of gifts, talents, powers, and intelligences of which you were unaware.

CHAPTER FIVE

CELEBRATION

"Celebrate endings—for they precede new beginnings."

—*Jonathan Lockwood Huie*
Quotes of Love, Celebration, Humor and Daily Inspiration

The celebration phase of the rites of passage is when the initiates are acknowledged for their successful completion of the initiation. They are celebrated by the community for acquiring the skills, attitudes, and values essential to becoming a young adult in their community. At the celebration, the initiates learn about the new privileges and responsibilities that they have earned through their mastering the required trials. The overarching premise of the celebration of the Rites of Passage Ceremony is for the community to affirm that each initiate who passes from one stage to the next is ready to do so, and that the community members comprehend and consent to the step being taken. Upon the completion of the ceremony, the initiate is held accountable for the responsibilities of young manhood as defined by his cultural values and community expectations.

Men Manifesting with Intention Celebration

In May of 2020, I received a text from the wife of one of my dear brothers sharing that I was nominated to receive an award and acknowledgement from the Spirit of a Woman (SOW) 2nd Annual Father's Day Celebration—"Fathering on Purpose: Men Manifesting with Intention." In response to the pandemic, SOW recognized the need to facilitate a daily virtual community healing space for Black Indigenous People of Color (BIPOC) through the Zoom platform entitled Wake Up Everybody (WUE). In honor of Father's Day 2020, the WUE community created a ceremony to salute fathers who are Living, Loving and Leading in alignment with their purpose. The eight honorees were identified as men who exhibit what it looks like to stand powerfully in their manhood, their leadership and their roles as fathers and father-figures in the community.

I was truly honored to be recognized by the WUE community that up to the time of the invitation I had limited awareness of, regarding the powerful work they were engaged in, curating for our community during the global pandemic. The virtual space provides a platform for the community to address trauma and issues that impede BIPOC people from living from the greatest expression of optimal health, particularly living through the omnipresence of oppression during the unprecedented times of the COVID-19 pandemic scare. I accepted the recommendation and began my onboarding process for the celebration. As I began to reflect on my life experiences as an educator, leader, Rites of Passage practitioner, keeper of African and Indigenous customs, ritualist, and an aspirant to the call to healing through Indigenous Spiritual Technology, I was grateful that a community saw value in my Divine assignment. I recognized how the web of connection has profound impact, as I was not a member of the WUE community, yet through my services, members of the village were familiar with my mission. Though I was not initiated formally or informally by the WUE community, it was by this community that I was being honored for the passages that I have experienced. It is important to recognize that the awareness of the rites of passage process helps us to locate where we are in our initiatory journeys. In formal experiences, the vision, mission, design, and practices follow a well-choreographed plan. However, when life experiences constitute your trials and initiation, knowledge of the rites of passage framework is invaluable as it helps us identify the trials and create meaningful narratives that help us cross thresholds and affirm when we have entered a new phase in our lives.

The WUE celebration came shortly after my Elemental Immersion initiation with Malidoma Somé. Though we had ample time to reflect, contemplate, and affirm each other during our trials, we did not have a formal celebration upon the completion of our initiation, nor did I celebrate upon my return home. From April to June, I was still unraveling and integrating the enlightenment that was cultivated by participating in these radical rituals. I drew a connection between the initiation that occurred with the elements and the "Fathers on Purpose" celebration. The Elemental Immersion initiation supported me with clarifying my purpose in the domain of healing and transformation. I returned home with a renewed sense of my calling, the gifts that I possess, and the "sacred medicine" that emanates through me, as me. The WUE ceremony was not only a celebration, but an introduction into the next stages of my purpose as a vehicle for healing through the Rites of Passage and Indigenous Spiritual Technology process. The WUE community offered me an invitation to deepen my *"innerstanding"* of myself as a healer and strip away all the filters and some of the conventional settings that had restricted me from executing due to policies and mandates that remove Spirit and sometimes ritual from the teaching and learning process. As the Elemental Immersion experience facilitated my metaphoric death and ignited my indwelling powers, the WUE Ceremony charged me to operate from an unadulterated intention to use healing modalities that are rooted in our African and Indigenous traditions and apply them to 21st century challenges and opportunities. It also ushered me into a community of healers who are called to share their "medicine (healing gifts and purpose)" and have a space for those who have embraced healing as their call to address their own wounds, fears, insecurities, and shadows in a safe and Spirit imbued setting. In short, my WUE Celebration was a call to the next phase of my healing initiation where I am currently experiencing trials that will prepare me to hone my gifts, learn new skills and reveal insights to the greater expression of my life as a vehicle for healing on the planet.

On the day of the event, I woke up around 5:30am as the WUE events begin at 7:00am. After the tech run was complete, the program started in the African customary ritual of granting permission from an elder to begin. Once consent was granted, we summoned the Ancestors through libations. The hostess, Shawnee Benton Gibson (Founder and Executive Director of Spirit of a Woman, Be the Tree Rites of Passage for Women and Executive Producer of Wake UP Everybody) shared the intention and rationale for the day. As the ambience was now set, each honoree's biography was presented by one of the WUE members. After the introduction, the honorees shared a brief narrative of their journey with an emphasis on the origins of their missions and the journey of cultivating their gifts, claiming their purpose, and their process to becoming.

After all the honorees shared their narratives, they were presented with a plaque with the name and image of an Ancestor who was chosen to inspire, support and continue to guide their mission. The Ancestor served as an exemplar to our community, the honoree's work and provided a road map to excellence. The Ancestor that was chosen for me was Dr. John Henrick Clarke, the preeminent erudite Scholar Warrior who devoted his life to countering the narrative of distortions propagated by European/White supremacist and racist notions of Black people's history. As a child, Dr. Clarke was told by one of his White teachers that Black people made no notable contributions to history and civilization. His Spirit resisted this insidious idea and set him on a mission to research the history, culture, and identity of African people and the African Diaspora. He was a master teacher who to this day is recognized worldwide as one of our premiere scholars. Dr. Clarke is a giant in African communities worldwide. I was deeply humbled by having my name associated with his amazing contributions. I will spend the rest of my life doing my best to impact our community through the Rites of Passage practice and by learning and sharing other sacred rituals, customs, and healing modalities. The charge by the WUE community and the gratitude for the contributions that I had made up to this point of my life have inspired me to continue to be fully present to my Divine assignment and to utilize all my gifts to facilitate healing, transformation and empowerment for my family, community, people, and world.

After the award was presented, the WUE community unmuted themselves and collectively shared their affirmations, gratitude, accolades and praise for me and the work that I have accomplished and encouraged me to continue my path. This process was done for all the honorees. It was an amazing tribute that I will always cherish.

As I received acknowledgement for the accomplishments of my mission through this community of healers and transformers, I also heard the invitational call to join the community and begin my initiation of deepening my facilitation and administering the sacred practice of rites of passage through the WUE process. Since the celebration, I have facilitated virtual workshops on the rites of passage framework and have learned new strategies for supporting individuals on their life paths through the rites of passage practice. I have never considered using the rites of passage framework as a life coaching strategy to support individuals in locating where they are within the rites of passage framework. The workshops that I have facilitated and the complementary consultations that I conducted afterwards, birthed a new function for the services that I provide. Additionally, through this new experience, I have joined the WUE administrative team which focuses on the Spiritual and technical skills of curating a virtual online platform with a healing sensibility and methodology. When you have chosen your path, Spirit has a way of directing you to your next initiatory experiences. I am now in a new space that enables me to continue to evolve on my path and learn new skills to execute my Divine purpose. Through WUE, I am fully engaged in the rites of passage process and blessed with the opportunity to acquaint myself with areas of vulnerability as I activate dormant qualities that would only emerge through dancing with fear, insecurities and challenging unproductive thoughts, emotions, and narratives.

Celebratory embrace from a Sankofa Passages facilitator upon the successful completion of the Young Men's Passage Experience
North Carolina Central, Durham, NC, 2012

Reflective Questions for *Jegnas* on Celebration

To maximize the ceremonial experience for the initiates, let's take some time to examine the ceremonies that have occurred in your life. All throughout the transformational journey of the boys and young men, it will be necessary to have a self-referencing point of your own relationships with the phases of becoming. In this reflection process, you will know how to use your experiences to establish meaning, value, empathy, and mindfulness of what the initiates will encounter as they prepare and go through their experiences and as you observe their growth.

The following are questions that will enable you to reflect on the formal and informal celebrations and ceremonies that have occurred in your life. Deeply ponder these events and answer as honestly as possible:

🌀 What were the trials you mastered that earned you the opportunity to be celebrated by an individual, family or community?

🌀 What new expectations, privileges, and responsibilities were you charged with living up to during the celebration? What were your thoughts about your new status?

🌀 Were you provided any artifacts that were symbolic of your transformation? What were the symbols? Explain their meaning.

🌀 Were there any rituals that symbolized your transformation from one stage of life to the next? Describe the rituals and their meaning. Describe what your thoughts and feelings were as you participated in these rituals.

🌀 Who were the people who were present at your ceremony? What role did they play at the ceremony? What special words did they share about you during the ceremony? Describe how you felt hearing and receiving the accolades and nourishing reflections.

🌀 What new expectations and assignments were you charged to demonstrate upon the completion of the ceremony? Who was going to hold you accountable for the new commitments and responsibilities that you were expected to carry out?

🌀 Did you share any words during the ceremony? What did you express? How did you feel about making a public declaration?

🌀 Upon the completion of the ceremony, did you feel prepared to re-enter back into your life with your newfound knowledge, values, and skills? Explain.

As elders, parents and Jegnas prepare for the ceremony, the following are the essential focal points that will be highlighted and addressed:

🌀 **Recognition of trials successfully mastered:** The adults in the ceremony will acknowledge the thresholds that they witnessed the young men cross and share narratives of what they

161

witnessed. *Jegnas* be mindful to **not** share what the trials were as it will lose its potency and spoil it for the younger boys who might be attending the ceremony. "What the eyes have seen, the ears have heard; and what the ears have heard, the eyes have seen," can be an enigmatic response given to any that make inquiry regarding our sacred trials and rituals.

Assign meaning to new privileges earned and responsibilities gained because of mastering the trials:
What does this process really mean for the young men who successfully went through the experience? The adults must have meaningful opportunities for the young men to exhibit their unfolding mission, new skills, leadership, intelligences, and sensibilities.

Symbolic acknowledgement of new position in the community:
What symbol will be assigned to make a distinction that the young men have been tried, tested, and approved as young adults in their community? What is the meaning of the symbol? When and where should they wear the symbol? For *Jegnas*, your symbolic offering may be a talisman (medicine pouch or necklace imbued with elemental materials).

Charge to live up to expectations of new status:
All of the adults participating in the ceremony should be clear on the values and expectations that they will be anticipating the young men to represent through their actions, words, and deeds.

Community charge to hold initiate/student accountable for new skills learned:
The community members in attendance will be fully engaged with call and response activities that will affirm and support the young men's declarations. Everyone in attendance is a witness to the formal transition from one stage of life to the next. This process also reminds the adults on how they must be conscientious of how they comport themselves in the public and model the virtues that the young men are expected to exhibit.

Designing the Rites of Passage Ceremony for Initiates

As *Jegnas* it will be significant to prepare the initiates for the final phase of their Rites of Passage experience. Having the initiates reflect on major paradigm shifts and the moments where they were able to summon their indwelling powers will help them to see their growth and affirm their capacity to endure, activate their will, locate their Spirit to confront adversity, creatively problem solve and strategically apply powers and intelligences that were lying dormant within. The exposure that they received during their initiation will culminate in their own assessment of their experiences. The following questions/prompts will help them to connect with the transformation that occurred and serve as a remembrance of what it takes to evolve, expand, and grow.

The following are some questions and prompts that will support them in crafting their Manhood Declaration Statements:

- Describe your thoughts and feelings when you first heard the call to initiation. Were you excited? Resistant? Scared? Indifferent? Angry? Curious? Explain.

- What were the greatest challenges for you during this initiation process?

- What did you learn about yourself during this experience? Share new gifts, talents, or interests. Also, share areas where you still need to grow.

- Who were the Jegnas that you connected with during this experience? Reflect on why you were drawn to them. What did their presence inspire in you?

- Describe some of the experiences that were breakthrough moments for you? How did these experiences impact how you view yourself, your community and life in general?

- As we prepare for our Rites of Passage celebration, share what you are most proud of about yourself? How do you plan to display the latest version of yourself?

As you prepare to return to your family and community with your new status, responsibilities, and privileges, what gifts will you share? How will our family, community, people, and world benefit from your presence?

(Left to Right) Donnel Jones, Salim Ptah, and Carlos Francis
Bolo Bolo Blauweh African Drumming Troupe led the
Walk of Integrity Processional Coalition of Schools
Educating Boys of Color 10th Annual Gathering of Leaders
Jacob Javits Center, New York City, 2010

The Rites of Passage Ceremony

Processional Drumming and Dance: The processional will be preceded by the drum call and the entry of dancers. The voice of traditional drum rhythms and the movement of dancers help guide the community to the present moment and establish the language of unity and collective identity. Experienced traditional folkloric drummers and dancers will know the appropriate rhythms to play for rites of passage ceremonies that are significant for setting the stage for the celebration.

As *Jegnas* prepare the young men for their final Walk of Integrity, they should remind them that they have displayed powerful achievements that have earned them the privilege to join the brother-hood of men in their communities. The *Jegnas* should beam with pride and let the young men know that the community must make the final decision on their acceptance of their right to enter the village as young men. The *Jegnas* will remind the young men that the community should see with each glide of their step that they have transitioned from boyhood to young manhood.

Intention for the Celebration and Welcoming/Opening Remarks:

The lead *Jegna* will welcome the participants with a brief statement on the vision for the ceremony. Prior to any other remarks, the *Jegna* will seek permission from the elders to begin the celebration. The following is an example of the protocol:

Permission from Elders:

The welcoming remarks will be followed by identifying the elders (identified prior to the ceremony as distinguished participants). The lead *Jegna* will establish the rationale for the ceremony and contextualize the significance and intentions for the gathering. The following is an example of the Elder's Consent Protocol:

Introduce the elders and have them stand in front of the venue (have a special table designated for them to sit). If they are not able to stand, they will remain seated. The lead *Jegna* will state the following prompts:

"To our esteemed elders, we seek your permission today to facilitate the Rites of Passage Ceremony in honor of our young men who have endured _____ months of initiation in their quest to be recognized as young men in our community."

"Do we have your consent?"

"Esteem elders are there any words of wisdom that you can offer to set a powerful ambience for today's ceremony? "

"Thank you elders for your blessings and support!"

Libation The following libation statement is contextualized for the closing ceremony.

The Lead *Jegna* will facilitate libation or request an elder, priest, Reverend, Minister, Imam, Spiritual Practitioner, etc.

Ritual Facilitator: "Infinite Spirit, we are grateful for your presence in this sacred moment. Thank you for ensuring that our tribute to the Ancestors is performed with the highest expression of Love and is executed with deep sincerity."

Village: *Ashe'* (Let it be so, and so it is)

Ritual Facilitator: "Great Ancestors, we welcome you into our ceremony today with extraordinary joy! Thank you for joining us as we celebrate and affirm the successful passage from boyhood to manhood."

Ritual Facilitator Pours Water.

Village: *Ashe'* (Let it be so, and so it is)

"Welcome caring loving, compassionate, wise, and recent bloodline Ancestors (deceased from the present to two hundred years ago). We are grateful that you are present today. We call your names and seek your guidance with helping to celebrate and charge our young men for their next sacred assignments.

We now call your names (participants call the names of their recent personal bloodline Ancestors)."

Ritual Facilitator Pours Water.

Village: *Ashe'*

Ritual Facilitator: "Welcome African and Indigenous Ancestors. The foundation and genesis of our bloodlines, we are grateful that you are present today. Ancient wise, compassionate, Loving, and brilliant Ancestors, we call your names to provide us with wisdom, guidance, and direction with celebrating and honoring our young men.

We now call the names of our ethnic groups, Indigenous homelands, and bloodline Ancestors from antiquity."

Ritual Facilitator Pours Water.

Village: *Ashe'*

Ritual Leader: "Welcome Community and Notable Ancestors who made it your mission to advance freedom and the greatest possibilities for people of African and Indigenous heritage. We are grateful for your presence today.

Powerful leaders, teachers, and guides, we now call on your brilliance, courage, visions, and missions with celebrating, honoring, and tasking our shining examples of young manhood."

Ritual Facilitator Pours Water.

Village Responds: *Ashe'*

Ritual Facilitator: "Welcome Spirit Life that will one day be our Future, The Unborn! We acknowledge your presence today. Future Beings, we promise to invest in creating the greatest conditions for optimal living on the planet. We pledge to you that these future fathers, grandfathers, great-grandfathers will establish a powerful legacy for you to inherit and pass on for generations to come. Future Ascendants, your attendance here today will help us envision where we desire to go. We will continue to work steadfast with your presence at the core of our hearts and minds."

Ritual Facilitator Pours Water

Village Responds: *Ashe'*

Acknowledgement of the Sacred ROP practice and its Necessity for the 21st Century: Why are We Here Today?

Once the elder grants permission and the Libation ritual is performed, the lead *Jegna* will set the stage by making "The Call."

The Lead *Jegna* or a designee *Jegna* will be assigned to make the call to the community. The following is a sample call for the celebration ceremony:

"Now that the Creator and our Ancestors are present, we call the community to grant permission for these initiated young men to return home and take their rightful positions as viable contributors to their families, our community, their people, and the world. Gleaning from the wisdom of antiquity, the rites of passage were established to ensure that we build a legacy aligned with our highest ideals. Today our sons return from their initiation as men prepared to contribute their powerful gifts and Divine purpose to our village and beyond. Our young men who have successfully mastered their trials are the ones that our Ancestors prayed would come to restore harmony, balance, and order in the world! We are grateful for their precious lives and that they demonstrated the courage, strength, perseverance, and knowledge that have earned them young adult membership within our community!

Our mission through this rite of passage process is to cultivate the brilliance in our young men and guide them to the threshold of their Divine purpose! As we speak, there is a narrative that has been normed in our society that our boys are flat lining in every area of life that represents success and adorning the gold medal in every category that represents failure! Our communities have fallen under the spell of a self-fulfilling prophecy of low to no expectations other than being monikered as the monsters of our society. Now, more than ever, it is essential for the age-old Indigenous process of transformation and becoming to be fully restored in our communities. Our boys and young men must be reconnected to Sankofa narratives that affirm their identity centered on their relationship with the African and Indigenous concept of self (which consists of the Divine, the Ancestors, their people's story, rituals, healthy interaction with nature and community, and an emphasis on their physical/emotional/ mental and Spiritual wellness). This Indigenous notion of the self, supported by healthy education and socialization experiences will give birth to a man with the Indigenous genius of antiquity who has the capacity to master and inno- vate the modern world with the unique creative style that resonates in his blood memory).

Today, we call on our community to celebrate our young men for their successful passage from boyhood to young manhood. They will need the community to remind and hold them accountable to our core virtues and the declara- tions that they make today. They will need you to be present with them as integrating these lessons can be extremely chal- lenging. They will need you to uphold the creed and prin- ciples by exemplifying them in your daily life walk.

Boys left our village; young men have returned! They are now prepared to take on leadership roles and model the virtues, skills and intelligences that reflect what the best of manhood looks like in our community. We offer heartfelt gratitude to the parents, the *Jegnas*, and the community at large for help- ing to harvest the brilliance in our promising young men.

Today, our village decides whether the young men are ready to take on their new assignment and execute it based on the criteria that represents our people's commitment to cultural excellence. They are now the personification of the unfolding pages of the Book of Life poem."

Jegna Shares Reflection and Introduces Young Men and Their Families

At this stage of the ceremony, the *Jegnas* will introduce each young man and their families (*Jegnas* will pre-select the initiates that they will introduce prior to the ceremony and prepare their reflections and remarks). The following is a guide that can be used for introducing and honoring the young men:

I now introduce _____ (young man)
and his parents/guardians_____.

When _____ started his initiation, he was_____ (Describe his attitude, behaviors, characteristics). Over the course of the initiation, I have witnessed _____ _____ (Speak to his growth and transformation). I am proud of _____ for _____ (Personal and academic achievements). As a community, I can assure you that we can expect _____ _____ from our young Warrior King, _____.

As the young man approaches the stage, he is accompanied with his parents/guardians. They will have a cord that surrounds them, and their son will be attached to the end of the cord. When they reach the front of the stage, the Lead *Jegna* will sever the cord with scissors. This "Cutting the Cord" ritual symbolizes the second umbilical cord being detached. It signifies his separation from dependency as a child on his parents. He now begins to establish a new relationship as a young man that takes on greater responsibilities and commits to collaborating and co-creating experiences that support his new status as a young adult in his community. He is now a contributor to his family's work to build legacy, and his community's advancement through the contribution of his evolving purpose. Once the cord has been cut, the parents/guardians will honor their son. The following can be used as a guide:

Greetings! We are the parents/guardians of _____
_____. We represent the _____
_____ (Identify bloodline lineages). As a boy, our son has been _____ (Describe the gift that he has been to your family. Mention his qualities and what he contributed as a child). During your initiation I have watched you _____
(Describe his growth, achievements, and proud moments). As you have entered this chapter of manhood, we are excited and anticipate that you will _____
_____ (Vision for your son's manhood journey).

Once the parents honor their son, one of the *Jegnas* will guide the initiate to the podium to make his declaration. The *Jegnas* will cleanse him with sage as a symbolic purification and entry through a portal to a new chapter. This ritual is well known in many African and Indigenous cultures. The smoke from the sage helps release any negativity from the energy field of a person or space. As the young men are about to enter their new assignment, they will begin from a place of Spiritual, mental, and emotional clarity with an unobstructed path to the next chapter of their personal journeys.

Once the young men are introduced, it is their time to state their Oaths. The following is a framework that can be used to express their declaration:

I AM A YOUNG MAN OF THE PAST LIVING IN THE PRESENT

MOVING TOWARDS THE FUTURE

MY NAME IS _____, the son of
_____.
Today, in honor of _____
_____, I make a commitment
to_____.

During the last _____ months/year of my
initiation, my greatest lessons have been _____
_____. As a young man, I am now ready
to exhibit _____.

After experiencing initiation, I am clear that manhood means
_____.

As a representative of my family and community, I know that
I am expected to _____.

I want to acknowledge _____
_____ (List the names of people you would like to
recognize who have been influential in life and during your
initiation).

As a legacy builder committed to building for eternity, my
Divine gifts and purpose will impact the world by_____
_____.

At the conclusion of each Declaration of Manhood statement, the
Lead *Jegna* will request consent from the elders and community to
affirm the young man's Oath. The protocol should sound something
like this:

Lead *Jegna*: Wise Elders and beloved community members,
_____ (name of young
man) has shared his Oath as a declaration of his commitment to living according to the Divine design of his life and

contributing his gifts to his family, community, people, and world. Has _____ earned the privileges and responsibilities of young manhood in the _____ _____ community (name the community)?

Elders and Community Response: *Ashe', Ashe', Ashe'* (Let it be so and so it is) or *Rara* (No).

At this time the young man's father, or father figure, will gift the young man with something symbolic to acknowledge his new status in the community of men. The following are gifts that can be presented:

- Talismans created with materials that represent the young man's Ancestral legacy, life purpose, goals, with culturally protective amulets).
- Necklaces, bracelets, or rings with the sacred symbol of the organization or family emblem.

After the young men have been formally acknowledged and affirmed, the last statement of their intention will be expressed through a freestyle dance, step, poem, or song that conveys their new identity as young men in the community. Whatever is agreed upon as the creative expression must allow for each young man to share their distinctive identity through a solo. The following are some suggestions for the creative rendition of their presentation:

- Freestyle Cypher (The theme of their freestyle can be "Minute by minute/Hour by hour/As we know Our Story/We Know Our Power or "I'm a man of the past, living in the present, moving towards the future." This is an improvisational expression that doesn't have to rhyme; there should be music to create the ambience and portal for community connection and collective ethos.

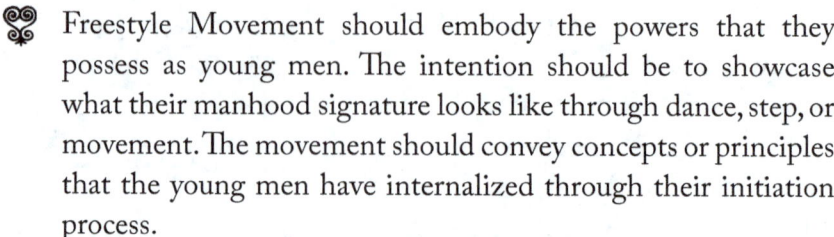

Freestyle Movement should embody the powers that they possess as young men. The intention should be to showcase what their manhood signature looks like through dance, step, or movement. The movement should convey concepts or principles that the young men have internalized through their initiation process.

If you feel that your young men will have difficulty performing these exercises on the spot, the *Jegnas* should prepare them for this presentation yet leave an element of improvisation within the rehearsed plan. It is important that they continue to embrace the unexpected with full present-moment awareness as life often presents unforeseen events that can serve as entry points to activating dormant gifts that only unique situations can bring forth.

After the presentations, the Lead *Jegna* will charge the community from the date of the celebration forward to be present for the young men as they integrate into their families and communities as young adults. It is the community's responsibility to invite the young men to opportunities that are aligned to their unfolding missions and hold them accountable to their oaths and new ways of thinking, knowing and being. Most importantly, the community must be intentional about modeling the core values and practices of what healthy adulthood looks like in the community and continue to commit to their continued transformation and reincorporation process.

Young Men Recite "Book of Life" Poem by Haki Madhubuti

The "Book of Life" poem represents concepts, virtues, ideals, instructions, and practices for optimal Black manhood. When the poem is ritualized it serves as a barometer for making daily decisions that are aligned with healthy principles that will ground and support boys and men in assessing themselves and providing a blueprint for their manhood journey.

At this time of the ceremony, have the *Jegnas* and the young men recite the poem together and encourage the young men to engage with the poem in their ritual practices and reflective time.

"BOOK OF LIFE"
Haki Madhubuti

You will recognize our brothers by the way they act and move throughout the world.
There will be a strange force about them,
There will be unspoken answers in them,
This will be obvious not only to you but to many.
The confidence they have in themselves and in their community will be evident in their quiet saneness.

The way they relate to women will be clean, complementary, responsible and with honesty.
The way they relate to children will be strong and soft,
Full of positive direction.
The way they relate to men will be that of questioning our position in this world,
Will be one of planning for movement and change,
Will be one of working for their people,
Will be one of gaining and maintaining trust within their community,
These brothers at first will seem strange and unusual.
But this will not be the case for long.
They will train others and the discipline they display will become a way of life for many.
They know that this is difficult, but this is the life that they have chosen for themselves, for us, for life:

They will be the examples,

They will be the answers,

They will be the first line builders,

They will be the creators,

They will be the first to give up the pleasures,

They will be the first to share a value system,

They will be the workers,

They will be the scholars,

They will be the providers,

They will be the historians,

They will be the doctors, lawyers, educators, farmers, priests, and all that is needed for development and growth.

You will recognize these brothers and

THEY WILL NOT BETRAY YOU!!

Closing Remarks Elders and Lead *Jegna*

As the ceremony concludes, the Lead *Jegna* and/or an Elder will acknowledge the young men, their families, the *Jegnas*, the Elders and the Ancestors for co-creating a powerful initiation and Rites of Passage experience. The young men will be given a last charge that should sound something like the following:

"You have showed mastery over the trials; you have internalized our core values, you have cultivated dormant strengths and you have become competent, confident, conscientious, and exhibited commitment. You have taken bold steps toward actualizing your mission! It's now time for you to join your community as young men and unleash your purpose and gifts as we work towards continuing to build a legacy that will last for eternity. It is now time to take your rightful post in this world and let your Divine purpose and gifts shine! As a Spiritual presence that lives and moves as you, our community welcomes you into your new identity as men of the past, living in the present and moving towards the future.

Lastly, the young men will close by leading a call and response mantra. The following is a recommended mantra:

"Sharpen your eyes.
Tune your ears.
So, you know what you see.
Understand what you hear.
Minute by minute
Hour by hour
As we know Our Story
We know Our Power!!!

Ashe', Ashe', Ashe'

Young Men's Exit Processional Ritual

The young men will lead the exit procession out followed by their families, the Elders and the Jegnas. The significance of the young men departing first denotes the expectation of their responsibility to lead and be the first to clear the way for the community. The drummers will play an up-tempo celebration rhythm as everyone exits.

Suggested rhythms: Dununba, Kuku, Dansa and Soko

Clean Up Ritual

In the Spirit of leaving our community more beautiful and beneficial than we inherited, Kuumba, there should be a selected clean-up crew available to ensure that an effort is made to leave the space in a better state than when it was received.

CHAPTER SIX

REINCORPORATION

"True initiation never ends."

—*Robert Anton Wilson*
Tale of the Tribe: Scrying for Shards

The post-ceremony phase is known as reincorporation, implying a return to the essence of oneself. Upon reentry, one crosses the threshold into adulthood, reconnecting with the familiar world yet imbued with newfound wisdom. No longer joined to childhood innocence, the individual perceives their new life through the lens of proven maturity, evidence of the transformative journey undertaken.

The reincorporation phase begins upon the successful completion of the passage experience. The young men are now poised to play a formal leadership role in their communities. Upon the return to their communities, they contribute to helping influence decisions, particularly in the areas where they have exhibited mastery or a deep interest in a discipline. They enjoy new privileges and embrace responsibilities. By virtue of their initiation, they are great candidates to serve in helping guide others through the passages to being exemplary young men.

As the young men integrate back into life with their families and community, it is important to know that his *new initiation* begins as soon as he leaves the ceremony. He will need time to integrate all the profound wisdom and experiences that he learned during his formal initiation process. The young men will still need guidance with executing their new roles and responsibilities, and learning how to be proper managers of their earned privileges and powers. The *Jegnas* and Elders will need to still make themselves available for the young men, help guide them through more thresholds and support their overall health, wellbeing, and transformation process. Some of the trials that they experienced may be seen as isolated and germane only to the moment of their initiation; yet through establishing monthly or quarterly meetings with the group that crossed thresholds together, their experiences can be transferred to the new trials and ordeals that life will present to them. It will be important to remind them of the powers that were manifested through the experiences that they went through collectively and have the *Jegnas* and their brothers hold a reflective mirror up to them as they reincorporate themselves as leaders and young men in their communities. During these reunions, the young men explore the multiple ways that they can be of service and integrate their gifts and purpose, as well as examine their thoughts and emotions that have arisen upon their return. Furthermore, it holds profound significance for young men to make a solo visit to the site of their initiatory trials, engaging in a ritual or ceremony that resonates with their current mental, emotional, and spiritual states. This act serves as a deeply personal acknowledgment of transformation and growth, honoring the unique journey each person embarks on.

The essential message that *Jegnas* must convey to the young men who have re-entered and are navigating the reincorporation state is:

Life is experienced in rhythms of high and low, that the ascent of every mountain top is followed by descent, that highs and lows are interdependent and necessary for the growth of the self. Every Spiritual tradition reminds us of the inevitability, even the necessity of the darkness that follows illumination. The trail ahead can be taken at your own speed. You don't have to have everything figured out. Your ability to pursue your vision for your life does not depend on how fast you are or how resolved your picture of the universe is. What does matter is your ability to persevere. The initiation and the threshold time was a test of your ability to persevere (Mahdi, Foster & Little p. 106).

(Left to Right) David Vandiver, Stan Ellison, Dr. R.A. Ptahsen Shabazz, Kamau Ptah & Leonard Townes. Harambee Rites of Passage Group Facilitators. All these men returned to their communities bearing extraordinary gifts from their postsecondary academic initiations.
Theodore D. Young Community Center, Greenburgh, NY, 1996

The Return from Hampton University

As I was standing in the processional line for the graduation ceremony, I was reflective about the profound transformation that took place in my five years at Hampton University. In that moment, those who were in my family and circle of Love held a mirror to me that beamed with pride about reaching this stage of my journey. It all seemed surreal as I was preparing to embark on the next chapter with clear values, new skills and, most importantly, a voice that would help me to execute my mission as a young man on the "Know Thyself" path.

As I waited to enter the Hampton Coliseum, I took in the phenomenal view of all the graduates who were about to cross the threshold and be reincorporated into life with their newly developed skills, hopefully a sense of purpose and indelible memories of their college passages. As I was taking in all the joy of the moment, one of my close African Studies Cluster (ASC) brothers approached the line to greet me. He was all smiles and resonated with genuine excitement for me as we experienced similar self-created formalized passages during our years together. His presence was significant to me as our paths were paved with intense trials that helped to establish a view of life that was not always in alignment with the Hampton University Pirate mission and practices. In fact, we were often at odds with the University as we were a constant reminder and challenge to the institution to remember that cultural identity work was vital to our healing, transformation, and elevation as a people. My brother's presence was a recognition that the commencement ceremony would not capture and fully represent our paths at Hampton, which were met with resistance to our mission to restore our roots, culture, Indigenous intelligences and prepare ourselves to return to our communities with the capacity to heal and restore our people to their traditional greatness. From our perspective, the institution was preparing us to be cogs in wheels to sustain and maintain the American status quo. We were to continue to perpetuate the White Supremacy culture as batteries to advance the powers that benefit from our role as compliant laborers that would keep their (White wealthy corporate structures) systems alive and thriving. In fact, that was the original design of the institution that was founded by Samuel Chapman Armstrong.

My need to comprehend Hampton's resistance to the "Know Thyself" path led me to author my thesis paper on its founder entitled, The Philosophies and Opinions of Samuel Chapman Armstrong. My educational journey at Hampton was unsettling and I needed to know the origin of the thinking and values that had been creating such internal turmoil for me and those who came to Hampton seeking to be educated for liberation and cultural coherence. Armstrong inherited much of his philosophy about education from his father, Richard Armstrong who was Hawaii's Minister of Education and who emphasized student labor as a key component of schooling. Richard Armstrong was a missionary sent by the American Board of Commissioners for Foreign Missions to "civilize" the Nuka Hiva Polynesian and other Aboriginal ethnic groups. He established several churches and schools and was known as the father of American Education in Hawaii. Influenced by his father, Samuel Armstrong in collaboration with the Freedman's Bureau and the American Missionary Association founded the Hampton Normal and Agricultural Institute in 1868. Hampton evolved into a preserve for practical learning, where Black students were encouraged to prioritize personal growth and financial empowerment over political engagement. Both men's views were rooted in their beliefs that Whites were superior. Fundamentally, the motivation of the Hampton Model was designed to produce a cadre of Black laborers who would work to ensure that the northern textile industries were thriving. Additionally, it was created to train "an army of Black educators" who internalized the ideals of self-improvement and job training to enable Black students to become gainfully employed and self-supporting as craftsmen or industrial workers. The contemporary rendition of the Hampton model can be expressed as a factory designed to produce labor for corporate America. This was quite evident at the Career Market and Recruitment Fairs, which sometimes resembled modern day auction blocks where students got "suited and booted" and prepared to generate wealth for major corporations, sometimes at the expense of their people's own best interest.

As we worked diligently to establish what our Ancestors called us to create through the ASC, my comrades and I were able to design African-centered frameworks and practices that provided us with the tools that would empower us to bring valuable gifts to the communities that we were returning home to serve. As I reflect on the experience, the opposition from Hampton was the necessary trial that would equip us with the ingenuity, sensibilities, and capacity to navigate the new terrain that we were entering upon our reincorporation into our next chapter.

As the graduation song, *Pomp and Circumstance* was played to begin our ceremony, I remember my ASC brother looking me in my eyes with honor and affirming, "the world is about to become a better place." I internalized that call as a charge for me to remain true to the formal and informal initiations that we had experienced together. It was a befitting statement to walk with and set the stage for receiving my degree and beginning my journey as a *Jegna* Initiate. As I entered the Coliseum, I focused on the people (students, family, and faculty) who were significant in supporting and guiding me in the direction of where my Spirit was pulling me. I took a deep breath and relished in the gratitude for the Love and the direction that I received. In that moment, I was appreciative for every experience that crafted my "Becoming" narrative.

Once the ceremony ended, my family and I went to have a meal and then packed the rest of my items to return home. As we journeyed back home, I recall receiving dreams and visions of what the next phase of my journey would look like, and messages began to download about a *greeting card line* that would convey distinct messages to students who were navigating the college experience. I thought about the encouraging messages that I received during my time in college and the ones that I crafted to members in my circle of Love. The Historically Black College and University (HBCU) experience is unique, and I was receiving messages that would speak directly to the hearts of those who were living and breathing the higher education passages and those who were connected to the students who were attending HBCUs. I also saw visions of myself working in my community, helping to establish powerful cultural education and socialization systems imbued with concepts and practices that cultivated our indigenous gifts, intrinsic intelligences, and ways of knowing, thinking and being.

Upon my return, I applied for a Social Studies teaching position at my alma mater Woodlands Jr./Sr. High School. I was excited, nervous, and apprehensive about pursuing a career at my old school, particularly as I was rooted in African-centered educational philosophies and practices that I knew would challenge the normed status quo of miseducation and Eurocentric indoctrination. Woodlands was a truly diverse community that prided itself on its liberal philosophy. I must say that the Greenburgh School District made efforts to create a school culture that reflected the diversity of the community, however it missed the mark as many public educational institutions perpetuate White supremacist doctrines through racist curricula and performance metrics that are not aligned to the cultural intelligences that children of African, Latino, and Indigenous people of color bring with them to the learning community. In fact, if it were not for the staff of conscientious Black educators, active Black parents and committed Black community members, by default Woodlands would have been like most other institutions where the students would have just fit into the learning environment instead of feeling a sense of belonging. As I reflect on my own experience as a student, I cannot say that the culture of the school made me feel at home. I was very connected to my peer group, a handful of teachers and my teammates on the track and basketball teams. As a community of Black, Indigenous, and Latino ancestry, we are consciously and unconsciously taught how to accommodate and create comfort and protection for White people who are not to be "burdened" by the dissonance of race, racism, and inequality. Many of our people were and still are sensitive to White fragility at the expense of our own self-interest. When the efforts of Black and Brown people are to ensure the emotional safety for self-identified Whites, it relinquishes the accountability for White people to be held responsible for their unconscious biases, micro-aggressions, and their sometimes very overt expressions of racism. I knew that where I was as a young man would challenge the quiet, voiceless, and well- admired non-threatening boy that departed just five years earlier.

When I arrived at the second interview, there was another Black man who was applying for the same position. He looked to be about 10 years my senior. I found out later in the interview process that he held a master's degree. His graduate work and professional experience gave him an advantage; my asset was being a celebrated son of Greenburgh, living and receiving my education there for 14 years at the time of my return from college. The second interview's trial was to simulate the lesson planning process by creating an eighth grade Social Studies lesson on any period in history from 1865-Present (at the time it was 1992). I was confident about this task, as for the past two years that is all I was doing in my student teaching, and observation and participation classes at Hampton. I recall designing a student-centered lesson on the Reconstruction Era that I felt was strong, particularly without any resources to support my planning process. As fate would have it, I was appointed as a Social Studies teacher for seventh and eighth grades. I was excited about my new venture and the beginning of my career path.

About two days after my interview, I was invited to meet the interim acting Superintendent, who was a Black man. He was very encouraging and hospitable. He recognized the significance of the impact that I could make as someone who returned to the community, particularly for the boys and young men who attended the school who could benefit from my presence and what my personal narrative could inspire. His words for me were welcoming and reassuring. He provided a presence of a fatherly figure who was aware of how essential it was to support a young Black professional entering into a system polluted by the poison of racism. I appreciated his sincerity and the time that he took to have a heart-centered conversation about the promise, possibilities and inherent challenges that would be a part of my next initiation. As I was about to leave his office, I noticed a beautifully framed poem on his wall. As I took a closer look, I recognized it was the poem that had served as a sacred text for me and my ritual journey to manhood and my "Know Thyself" passage. It was Listervelt Middleton's poem, "On the Origin of Things." I walked out of the office knowing that I had received a sign from Listervelt and my Ancestors that I was on the right path. I felt empowered to represent my authentic voice as a teacher imbued with the concepts and practices that I studied and internalized for the past eight years and was poised and ready to embark on my Divine assignment.

As I began my official journey, I commenced to put my teaching philosophy and practices to the test. I took it as a personal charge to breathe inspiration and provide multiple perspectives on the topics that were mandated in the Social Studies curriculum. During my first year, I spent a lot of sleepless nights seeking ways to decolonize the curriculum by invoking the historical presence and current events of the diverse students that were in my class. I utilized "Multi-Cultural Wheel Method," a concept that I learned from the renowned educator, Dr. Jawanza Kunjufu's professional development, which was a process that placed events at the center of the wheel and the spokes of the wheel reflected the ethnic groups that were involved in the event. The multiple points of view provided a context for how each group perceived and established a position on the event from their unique historical and cultural lenses. When students learned about the multiple perspectives, they were able to critically analyze the diverse viewpoints and derive their own comprehension about the events and how they impacted society then and now. This pedagogical approach was also married to a socialization process that I created as a classroom management practice. Gleaning from the ancient Nile Valley "Virtues of Ma'at" (Truth, Justice, Harmony, Balance, Order, Righteousness, Reciprocity, Propriety, Love), I established an accountability method for the class to hold each other responsible for exhibiting community principles that were designed to maintain a classroom setting that represented excellence. If a student was off task or disruptive, a member of the class would say, let's bring _____ (the person's name) into Ma'at. The entire class would hold up their hands in the Ma'atic posture (palms facing the distractor with the left hand in front of the right hand) and silently wait for the student to self-correct and return to their focus. The class knew the student was ready when he or she affirmed, "I am in Ma'at." This approach helped to create a classroom culture that shifted the primary focus of the teacher bringing order to the class, to students being able to maintain an environment that was conducive and appropriate for optimal levels of learning and engagement. The students had fun with making the hand gestures, often imitating Martin Lawrence's comedic hand motion when he was "checking" the characters Gina, Cole, Pam, and Tommy in the popular 1990s *Martin* sitcom. My reincorporation process was having an impact in supporting students with building a healthy self-concept and community sensibilities.

When authentic transformation occurs, it is bound to create some disturbance in a culture where community norms that perpetuate institutional racism exists. As I was establishing my presence and my mission began to unfold at the school, my trials of how to justify the practices started to come to a head. I was called into several meetings to defend my curriculum and teaching methods, particularly the classroom Virtues of Ma'at. I wasn't overly concerned as I was receiving outstanding teacher evaluations and was becoming well-respected by my colleagues and students. One day, the Social Studies department chairperson called me to meet with her to discuss a parent's concern about the Virtues of Ma'at. The parent was a Jamaican woman who was raising her son as a Christian and she interpreted the Ma'at refocusing method as an Islamic practice. The Jewish chairwoman inquired about this approach and asked, "are you teaching Islam." With complete comprehension of the fear and the culture of the school, which operated like this from the time I was a student until this meeting, I knew I had to quell the anxieties that were looming in the moment. I responded by saying, "I am not an Imam nor qualified to teach Islam and if I was, I know that as a Social Studies teacher that is not a part of the curriculum and my assignment." I continued by explaining the origins of the Virtues of Ma'at as being the "guiding core principles that helped to establish order, harmony and balance in ancient Nile Valley cultures" (*Ma'at: The Moral Ideal in Ancient Egypt*, Karenga p. 5). I then took liberty to assert that the Virtues of Ma'at are foundational tenets that influenced American democracy. The last statement was a stretch, yet I was determined to continue to defend what was contributing to a highly engaged and well-managed classroom atmosphere. Once she received my explanation, she assured me not to worry as she saw the value in what I was doing and would relate what she understood to the concerned parent.

In the school system, where White Supremacy culture has been normalized, any thought, act or affirmation of marginalized groups that counters the false narratives of the past and the pejorative notions of who people of African, Indigenous and Latinx people are translates to a declaration of war. At stake are the sensibilities of those who have races and cultures that have been affected by White Supremacy doctrines and who have internalized the intelligences, values and standards that are omnipresent in the institutionalized *racist* educational experience.

My reincorporation experience was an initiation into the trials of truly walking the "Know Thyself" path amid centuries of Eurocentric colonial miseducation systems designed to maintain the hegemony that affluent White men designed to establish legacies that maintained a power dynamic of "White superiority." My return home would be the beginning of a career that would venerate the Ancestral memory, voices, practices, and possibilities of who we were, are, and the affirmative vision of who we are destined to become while simultaneously destroying "Whiteness" as a worldview that has its origins in deception, lies, greed, and deep psycho-spiritual identity wounds.

My reincorporation and vocational initiation would continue at Woodlands with the facilitation of the young men's group (All Reaching in Search of Excellence – ARISE) established by my childhood friend and fictive big brother, the late-great Jonathan Mosely. Jonathan was also a son of Greenburgh and a product of the School District. He and my brother were best friends as children. He was also viewed as a treasured son returning home to contribute to the healing, transformation, and growing legacy of our community. Jonathan attended Hofstra University on Long Island and experienced a profound initiation through the New Opportunities at Hofstra (NOAH) Program, which helped to cultivate and refine his gifts as a leader. The NOAH Program was a culturally centered Rites of Passage that provided highly motivated and diverse students with access to higher education. The NOAH Scholars Program still exists and continues its mission to provide academic, financial, cultural, and social support resources for students from lower-socioeconomic backgrounds who attend Hofstra.

Jonathan was an exemplary scholar who personified the excellence that was expected of him and all the NOAH scholars. He was impacted and influenced by the then Director of the NOAH Program, Frank Smith. Jonathan carried the principles and practices internalized from the NOAH program and his family's community activism to design 'All Reaching In Search of Excellence' (ARISE). As Jonathan was devoted to ensuring that the young men at Woodlands had an opportunity to experience *Jegna* guidance from other Black and Brown men, ARISE served as a safe space for the young men in the learning community. The young men met once a week and discussed issues that impacted their daily lives and learned strategies that helped them to address their trials and take affirmative steps to overcoming obstacles and realizing their goals. The young men were encouraged to dress for success during the meeting days and they received powerful presentations from Black and Brown men from all levels of society on the tools, mindset, and strategies necessary to actualizing their vision and mission.

As Jonathan's mission started to pick up momentum, so did the opposition. His work and his impeccable character began to come under attack. He began to receive poor evaluations and he was perceived by the administration as an antagonistic presence. He was terminated from his position, and I was brought in as his replacement. He "schooled me to the game" but it was not enough for me to be able to avoid a similar fate. Learning from his narrative, I made sure that my classroom climate, culture, and pedagogy was flawless. As mentioned, there were concerns about my practice, as they were culturally inspired and applied to the modern teaching and learning experience. It was hard for the educational leaders and some teachers to accept anything that was effective, yet not learned through Eurocentric conventions and procedures.

My departure after three years at Woodlands was not a result of my performance, although I know at some point there was a strong probability that I would have journeyed the murky lot of intellectual and spiritual warfare that many strong, self-determined Black educators have experienced, before and after me. In fact, I would experience this through many phases of my career. After three years at Woodlands High School, I was released because of budget cuts. As the adage followed, the last one hired, the first one fired." Though there were significant efforts to defend and restore my position, I learned how powerless our voices were in the well-oiled machine of western education. I departed with great enlightenment and more determination to continue to be a vehicle for the reimagination of what effective teaching and learning should look and feel like for children of African, Latinx and Indigenous Ancestry.

As I carved out a space for the expression of my mission as a transformational educator at Woodlands, I also co-created a community-centered Rites of Passage initiative at the Fairview-Greenburgh Community Center (now known as the Theodore D. Young Community Center). The timing of the call to the community to launch the Harambee Rites of Passage Group, Inc. was appropriate as the negative issues that impacted male youth development were nationally on the rise. The conditions that are born out of institutional racism and White Supremacy culture are predictable in its destructive effect on Black and Brown communities. This reality as reflected in the mid-nineties, served as a portrait that illustrated our urgent need to address increased violence, gang activity, substance abuse, academic apathy, and anti-social behavior. The call to Harambee came at a time when the adult community, particularly men, were recognizing that the only way that these issues were going to be resolved was through the full commitment to restore our communities, especially the challenges that our boys and young men were facing. An undeniable factor that contributed to the awakening of men of African, Indigenous and Latinx Ancestry was the Honorable Minister Louis Farrakhan's call to the Million Man March. One year prior to the actual event, Minister Farrakhan launched a national tour that rallied, mobilized, organized, and informed communities about the current conditions that were impacting our communities, particularly Black men. Throughout the country, Local Organizing Committees (LOCs) were established to prioritize and address the issues that Black, Brown, Indigenous and Latinx communities were enduring. The Harambee call to action for our Greenburgh LOC was to establish a rites of passage initiative for boys nine to fourteen years old. The next chapter of my reincorporation phase was to lead a cohort of men from the community through a seven-month initiation to become rites of passage facilitators.

We had nine solid brothers who responded to the call and were trained to become Harambee Facilitators. The beauty of this experience was that most of the men were raised in the Greenburgh community and were able to reflect on our socialization experiences from the lens of rites of passage. We were able to think about the formal and informal trials that we all shared and envision an initiation that was informed by the healthy *and* harmful lessons that contributed to our transitions from boyhood to manhood. The facilitators' ages ranged from 26-46 years young. Most of us attended the same educational institutions and were influenced by the same teachers, coaches, artists, community leaders, bullies, sights, sounds and smells that were ubiquitous to our existence. For most of us, we were still in the initial stages of our reincorporation phase of completing our academic passage and returning with new gifts, talents, sensibilities, and intentions for advancing our communities. Out of all the rites of passage experiences that I have facilitated over the years, the Harambee stands as one of the most authentic as there already existed genuine bonds, connections, shared experiences, and rituals. Even where there were divergent perspectives of worldviews, strategies, and methods for socializing our boys, there was enough rooted experiences that were deepened through the training that created permanent bonds amongst the *Jegnas*. The rites of passage practice felt like it was the missing link to ensuring that there would be a great intention on curating practices, traditions and systems that would guarantee that the boys in Greenburgh would be ushered to healthy states of consciousness, confidence, and competencies to advance our community's culture and legacy.

As my reincorporation process continued, each leadership assignment led me to more roles, responsibilities, and trials. In addition to my teaching assignment, facilitation of ARISE and Co-Directorship for Harambee Rites of Passage program, I also served as an afterschool tutor at a homeless shelter. In my early adult mission, the community held up a mirror and continued to invite me to expand my unfolding mission as a cultural custodian, leader, transformational educator, and ritualist. I was often invited to speak or perform the opening ritual at Black History Month Celebrations, and I would facilitate Kwanzaa Celebrations during the Kwanzaa season. With each assignment that I took on I was presented with more trials that continued my initiation process. I learned through the reincorporation phase that it represents the new cycle of initiations. As we enter new roles, privileges, and responsibilities they present more opportunities to deepen our awareness, strengthen our skills, expand our capabilities, increase our confidence, and position us to summon the courage to take risks.

During the reincorporation phase, it is essential to stay connected to *Jegnas* and elders who have awareness and a context for the path that you are traveling. The guidance of the new terrains that you are navigating requires people who can help you to contemplate, motivate, strategize, and give you valuable guidance on your roles and responsibilities. If you have experienced a formal passage with *Jegnas* that you do not have direct access to, you will have to be amenable to embracing new advisors that know your path and can provide wisdom, encouragement, and a space for you to be vulnerable. When I returned from Hampton, I did not have direct access to some of the *Jegnas* that were a part of my college initiations, however, I was aware of my path and was able to identify members (elders and *Jegnas*) who would be able to continue to pour into my life and charge and challenge me to perform my responsibilities with the integrity that our Ancestors mandate for us to live and operate by. As I intentionally engaged my emerging purpose, Spirit and the Ancestors guided people and resources that would contribute to the unfolding and expansion of the mindset and tools that were necessary for each endeavor that I pursued.

Having knowledge of the patterns of transformation through the initiation process will help you with knowing what experiences you are going through and help you to identify how you need to compose yourself for whatever phase you are experiencing. My return from Hampton back to my hometown was a major entry point to more intense initiations (formal and informal) and life transformational events that ushered me to where I am in my mission today as a vehicle for healing, transformation, enlightenment, and the expansion of consciousness through the ancient system of rites of passage and Indigenous Spiritual Technology.

Sankofa Passages Warrior gives a reflection of his Young Men's Passage experience and shares his Oath. 7th Annual COSEBOC Gathering of Leaders Young Men's Passage University of Illinois, Chicago, IL, 2013

Jegna Reincorporation Reflections

Jegnas, let's take a reflective journey back to moments where you re-entered back into community life upon a formal (graduation, retreat, awards ceremony, public acknowledgement) or informal (random or unplanned acknowledgement of your character, gifts, talents, or growth) transformational experience. It is through a series of passages marked by ceremonies, that helped to establish your presence in community and allowed you to contribute valuable gifts, take on important responsibilities and offered you privileges based on your new status. In my experience, the reincorporation that occurs upon the completion of an initiation is often not as thoughtfully planned as the other phases and does not support the young adult in acclimating in their new role. The following questions will help you remember your reincorporation experiences and support you with creating the reincorporation process for the young men that you initiate:

- Describe your most significant formal or informal rites of passage experience.

- Upon the completion of your passage, what were you expected to do upon your reincorporation back to your family, community, career, or life endeavors?

- Once you returned to your community, describe how you exhibited your new position, status, and responsibilities?

- What *Jegnas* were supportive of you as you reincorporated back into the community? Were there any new Elders, *Jegnas* or guides that helped to facilitate your reincorporation?

- What privileges did you benefit from in your new position or status?

- What internal and external obstacles/trials did you encounter in your new position? How did you navigate these challenges?

- What unique contribution did you make to your community upon your return?

🔸 Describe the new cycle of trials that became a part of your next initiation upon your reincorporation.

🔸 Upon your reincorporation, how did your presence impact the community?

🔸 What lessons from your reincorporation experience will help guide you in supporting the reincorporation of young men into their communities?

Setting the Stage for the Return

Throughout the initiation there must be a concerted effort to identify and plan for the reincorporation of the young men. *Jegnas'* observations of their gifts, talents and emerging passions should be customized so that their growing purpose is at the center of their reincorporation. When planning their re-entry, it should not be done with a cookie cutter framework yet should take into full consideration the unique qualities, strengths, intelligences, and sensibilities that the young men contribute to the optimal health of the community. Sometimes what a young man has to offer by virtue of his gifts and purpose may not exist in the community. This would be the perfect time to organize the community to support the vision that the young man will need to birth from thought to reality.

The following are some suggestions to support the young men's reincorporation process:

🔸 Identify adults who are in vocations that the young men have expressed interest in pursuing.

🔸 Identify the different communities (schools, athletic teams, faith-based institutions, civic organizations, art programs, student government, etc.) that the young men belong to and share with the adult leaders the skills, qualities and attributes that were cultivated during their initiation. Share with the leaders the multiple ways that the young men that went through the rites of passage can contribute to their organization's mission based on what they learned during their initiation.

- Schedule post-rites of passage meetings to encourage the young men's reincorporation by providing technical skills to support their career paths and leadership platforms.

- Continue to check in monthly with the young men to discuss their post rites of passage learning plan, which should align with their Oath Statements, Vision Boards and other artifacts gathered to capture the essence of the men they envision becoming. After each meeting, have the young men identify action steps (trials) that they will take to manifest their visions and goals.

- Continue to invite the young men to community events and volunteer opportunities. This continued exposure will help them to crystallize their vision, identify their purpose and engage in the meaningful reflection of: Who am I? Whose am I? Where am I going? What's my purpose/mission? How do I get there? What skills must I learn? What mindset and values will help me to contribute my purpose in the most effective manner? How will my family, community, nation, and world be better because of my gifts and purpose?

Recommendations for Young Men Upon Their Reincorporation (Tips for Reincorporating)

Upon the completion of the rites of passage ceremony, it will be necessary for the young men to:

- Disengage for a day or two to reflect and integrate the entire experience, particularly the messages and the acknowledgments from the ceremony.

- Begin to review their oaths and establish goals for their reincorporation process.

- Establish new rituals that will support internalizing the manhood concepts, principles, and expectations of how to approach life with newfound awareness.

- Establish time to meet with the brothers that experienced the passage together. The rituals, trials and enlightenment that occurred is not something everyone in their daily interaction will comprehend. Their brothers will be able to "see them" in ways that the uninitiated person doesn't have the perception to notice.

- Return to where trials and rituals took place and bring some of their dilemmas to these spaces. Perform rituals, ceremonies, examine their hearts and contemplate their thoughts and emotions.

- Make a list of all the new trials that are a part of their new initiation. Journal about what thoughts and emotions are emerging as they live and learn through these experiences. Capture their highlights, insights and "aha" moments that reflect their enlightenment.

- Be available to share and celebrate their accomplishments. Not everyone will value their growth and they will sometimes have to acknowledge themselves when thresholds are crossed. They can call on their *Jegnas*, brothers, and other members who make up their sphere of obligation and influence to recognize major milestones that they have achieved.

- Make themselves available to attend the reunions and meetings with the *Jegnas*. This will deepen the reincorporation process as the *Jegnas* will continue to connect the dots and provide guidance, wisdom, and encouragement.

- Help support the *Jegnas* with the next cycle of initiates. Their presence will be valuable for the next group that experiences the initiation. Also, they will be reminded of their own grit, perseverance and becoming process and it will positively serve them in their reincorporation phase.

Sankofa Passages
Young men visiting Howard University (HBCU)
on a college and cultural excursion
Washington, DC, 2013

CHAPTER SEVEN

CONCLUSION

A s Indigenous people throughout the world experienced nature in an intimate manner, it can be reasoned that nature was the first curriculum that inspired *Jegnas* (facilitators of deep transformation). The question of how these original cultures created initiation rites that utilized similar practices is a mystery. How were these sacred knowledge systems and transformative disciplines choreographed and facilitated in similar ways when people lived remotely in their isolated communities? There was no email, social media, or authors writing and disseminating information about how to design and implement initiation rites. I lean to the theory that these early cultures crafted practices through their daily interaction with nature that surrounded their ecosystems. The elemental landscape as a teacher taught fundamental concepts about the nature of change and transformation. Through a deep relationship with the cosmos and elemental forces through daily living and rituals, original people throughout the globe received profound messages about the "becoming" process and translated nature's curriculum into the methodology for human initiatory rituals, protocols, and practices. Learning from nature provided consistent and reliable content that when integrated into the human experience, provided access to optimal methods for relating to and engaging with the environment. Nature gave birth to the initiatory rites practice, and therefore similar experiences simultaneously took place throughout the world. It will be valuable for *Jegnas* to engage in ritual practices and trials together in nature to receive guidance from nature's faculty.

Crossing the Threshold; Embracing the Call derives from an Ancestral call and deep yearning to restore the fundamental concepts that originate from the universal ancient tenets of initiation and rites of passage. The restoration of these principles and practices will help address the modern conditions that people of African and Indigenous Ancestry encounter, thereby supporting their healing, transformation, and activation of Divine purpose as the essential remedy to heal the issues that impact our family, communities, and the world. The effective application of these practices will set our communities on a path to using our innovative cultural modalities and spiritual technologies to contribute to a world that needs humanizing methods that speak to what it means to be Spirit incarnated in the human experience. Through African, Aboriginal, and Indigenous Spiritual and community-building technology, the aspirants of these ways of knowing and being will be poised to lead the planet and guide communities through transformational disciplines that help people realize what it means to live as Spiritual beings having a human experience created to achieve optimal levels of identity, community, and purpose-driven lives.

Crossing the Threshold; Embracing the Call initiation is intended to focus on the rites of passage practice to support those who hear the call to be *Jegnas*. I strongly recommend further studies on how Indigenous communities, historically and presently initiate, educate, and socialize their children. This will allow *Jegnas* to glean insight on conceptual frameworks, community centered values, symbols, folklore, archetypes, ritual practices, trials of enlightenment and the overall ethos and stylization of traditional initiation rites. The knowledge of these concepts and practices will help generate ideas for the initiations that you create.

Crossing the Threshold; Embracing the Call offers a framework to engage our communities in determining the pillars, values, norms, and systems that will ensure the healthy cultivation of intrinsic intelligences and sensibilities that are rooted in our cultural ethos. Our Indigenous traditions placed a high value on maximizing our Spiritual gifts and providing pathways for those gifts to be expressed as purpose for the greater good of community, which called for harmonious relationships with the Divine, Nature, Ancestors, Community, and Legacy. The work of the modern-day *Jegna* is to restore the African/Aboriginal/Indigenous "medicines" (cultural modalities, traditions, customs, rituals, folklore, ceremonies, elemental acknowledgements, concepts, values, songs, knowledge and Being systems, etc.) of our Indigenous Ancestors and creatively apply these practices to design the optimal Spiritual, mental, emotional, and physical health for the modern-day descendants. The charge for today's *Jegna* is reflected in Ayi Kwei Armah's book *Two Thousand Seasons*, when it was recognized that our Ancestors would no longer be in the comfort of our native environments and must remember and carry our traditions in new and strange lands:

> "Remembrance has not escaped us. Trapped now in our smallest self, we, depositories of the remembrance of the way violated...we fraction that crossed mountains, journeyed through forests, shook off destruction only to meet worse destruction: we, people of the fertile time before these schisms; we, life's people, people of the way, trapped now in our smallest self, that is our vocation: to find our larger, our healing self, we the Black people." (Armah, 32).

As we continue to navigate through the global initiation expressed as the ongoing threats of viruses, diseases, mental health challenges, climate shifts, environmental concerns, wildfires, and incessant systemic racism, how will our communities utilize the trauma, isolation, trials, and enlightenment that we experience as fuel to launch our celebrations and reincorporation back into society? How will our collective narratives and the awakening to the times that we are navigating help to inform our greatest priorities, particularly as it relates to the identity formation, education, and socialization of our children? As we re-imagine our initiations, passages, rituals, values, and legacies, what from our customs and practices should we bring into this new paradigm, and what mindsets and conventions no longer have value in the world that we are envisioning for ourselves? These are the critical questions that will help to inform the planning and design of our formalized initiation rites.

As I bring closure to this twenty-year project, I am intentionally embracing the next chapter of my journey with a greater mission to claim my existence as the highest expression of my Divine calling. I am bringing closure to every narrative that carries the burden, weightiness, and powerlessness of being a victim or having a victim mindset. I accept with gratitude that I chose to be on the planet at this time in the vessel of a copper toned, melanated Indigenous body to contribute to the expansion of human consciousness and to the optimal Spiritual, mental, emotional, and physical health of all who I am called to serve. I no longer view my existence from a victim mindset and storyline that White Supremacy culture and institutional racism are the unassailable barriers that determine my destiny. I am not in denial that these ideas and structures exist globally, however, I acknowledge and now make decisions that represent my highest and aspirational vision, which is not determined by the false narratives of an insecure, fear driven illusion of a birthright superiority and projection of itself on the world and the imprints that it leaves on the psyche of those who accept the narrative of this programming. In the past, I have always vehemently looked to justify the self-destructive behaviors of African, Black, Indigenous people to the internalized wounds of being victims of White Supremacy, racism, miseducation, colonized religion, and the media onslaught of programmed images that give birth to self-hatred along with destructive and powerless notions of the self. Again, these narratives are justifiable claims for the existence of negative behaviors in the cultures that have experienced these traumas. As I am clearer about my Divine assignment, I now choose to create sacred initiation opportunities through radical rituals that primarily support with reconnecting people of African and Indigenous Ancestry to their Divine contracts and higher purpose. My work will continue to guide our people to the threshold of their identities as Spiritual beings incarnate in the cultures that they are born into and create opportunities to remember their original contracts (Divine Purpose). The initiations will guide the aspirants to and through the narratives, thoughts, egoic attachments, and beliefs that are impediments to the actualization of the greatest version and highest expression of who we truly are as representatives of the Creator (Source, Most High, the Divine). Intellectualism alone cannot destroy racism. Theoretical and scholarly analysis cannot destroy racism. Having a deep faith or Spiritual practice alone cannot destroy racism. Violence cannot destroy racism. I don't purport to have the answer to eradicate racism and White Supremacy, yet I know that addressing it at its core will lead to not only analyzing the origins of race as crafted by White scientists that created the field known as race science and eugenics. Still, it will be necessary to put out a call to the human family to participate in radical rituals and bring this enormous dilemma to the Spirit of the cosmos and elemental powers (Earth, Fire, Water, Minerals, Air and Nature) where the release of this poisonous disease into nature's portals could create a deep rooted Soulful, Spiritual, and mental paradigm shift and alchemy that transforms this societal cancer to the optimal levels of Spiritual, mental, emotional, physical and global restoration. The other healing initiations and rituals can also be facilitated with the use of plant medicine. Again, it is about creating the intentions and bringing the world's most challenging issues that have imprinted themselves into the cellular memory and psyche of the modern-day human and applying Indigenous Spiritual Technology to support with optimal levels of healing and memory recall. These types of initiations are calls that will be made for those who are genuinely sincere about being vessels for healing of the planet and preparing humans for the New Earth. Eckart Tolle defines A New Heaven and A New Earth as the following:

"The foundation for a new earth is a new heaven—the awakened consciousness. The earth—external reality—is only its

outer reflection. The arising of a new heaven and by implica-
tion a new earth are not future events that are going to make
us free because only the present moment can make us free.
That realization is the awakening. Awakening as a future
event has no meaning because awakening is the realization of
Presence. So, the new heaven, the awakened consciousness,
is not a future state to be achieved. A new heaven and a new
earth are arising within you at this moment, and if they are
not arising in this moment, they are no more than a thought
in your head and therefore not rising at all. What did Yeshua
(Christ) tell his disciples? 'Heaven is right here in the midst
of you." (p, 307-308)

Those who are embracing the radical initiations are re-wiring and
re-engineering their life systems by purging traumas that are lodged in
parts of their body and activating dormant memories of their original
Spiritual and mental blueprints, creative designs, and original contracts.
These initiates are internalizing a new way of being that is having a
ripple effect as they reincorporate into their families, communities, and
circles of Love and influence. They are carriers of powerful energies,
practices, and healing modalities that create new ways of knowing and
being. Through these radical initiations, new intelligences, and sensibilities are awakening, and the notion of race is being experienced in a way
that is not governed by fear, hatred, separation, insecurity, hierarchy,
and trauma. The new lenses and mirrors are birthing the expression of
unconditional Love, peace, joy, abundance, acceptance, creativity, harmony, balance, Divine order, and purpose.

My personal initiations are now centered on remembering our
Soul contracts. This identification with the timeless NOW and infinite
powers completely eradicates the notion of race as the primary way to
define the self. As I type these words, I am summoning the awareness
of what the embodiment of this consciousness fully means. I am now
being called to matriculate out of the matrix that is rooted in the sym-
biotic relationship that reflects the historic struggle and patterns that

has so-called Black and Indigenous people fighting for equality with so called White people and the illusion of White superiority. In this shift of consciousness, I am still smack dead in the liminal phase of who I once was and who I am now becoming. I fully embrace the vulnerability of this transition as I am being prepared to sever the chords of the programs and conditioning that are impediments to my Spirit's greatest expression and what I now see as the treadmill relationship cycle of perpetrator and victim identification. As I am transitioning from a third dimensional reality to a fourth and fifth dimension, I am devoting myself to radical healing rituals and Soul retrieval practices to activate the dormant intelligences that yearn to be identified, acknowledged, and deployed. If this all sounds like a hodgepodge to you, it may be due to not fully integrating what some of my recent initiations have revealed and perhaps your inability to separate from an attached position, and fixated lens of life. For anyone who has experienced radical rituals, there exists a time where you connect with the oneness of all of creation. You become one and see your reflection in all animated life force. You also connect with concepts and ideas that transcend the ego's interpretation of identity and reality. For those who have known me throughout my life journey, this paradigm shift may come as a surprise, as for many years I have devoted most of my life to raising Black consciousness through African centered education. As I type these words, I too am observing what comes through with astonishment and wonder. It's like when I stood in the line for my name change, I am beckoning the call of my Soul's yearning and being pulled to where my Spirit is guiding me and stepping away from what is familiar, safe, and predictable. I absolutely Love the avatar that I have entered the world as, and I am grateful for all my experiences that have guided me to this NOW moment. I am trusting the process and heeding the call to personify the highest manifestation of the Divine in the bodies (Spiritual, Ancestral, mental, emotional, and ethereal) of Kamau Tehuti Ptah. My new declaration is not a severance from my cultural identity, yet it is an expansive and watcher's perspective of my life and some of the realms that I am being invited to enter cannot have attachments to the way that we define ourselves on the third dimensional plane of existence. To gain greater access to what the Spirit of the elements, plants, and cosmos must share, I will not be able to fully benefit from the journeys with a strong ego attachment to my earthly ways of interpreting reality. Though we as an original people have been assigned as synonymous with Soul, the Soul does not process life in the same manner as a human. When engaging in the higher realms of Spirit, the earthly ego identity dissolves and dies.

Through the activation of my blood and bone memories and the narrative of my Divine assignment, *Crossing the Threshold* has been a work of 30 years of study and practice using the transformative discipline of rites of passage. This work has lived wherever I was assigned the responsibility of being a *Jegna* for our children. Most of my assignments were behind what I considered "enemy lines," which required me to design approaches that operated in institutions governed by White Supremacy culture. The work sometimes took on the expression of what Capoeira became on plantations and what Santeria became by masquerading African Spirituality in the European version of Christian Catholicism. Both found ways to creatively undermine the racist institutions and provide a clandestine approach to connecting and remembering our sacred practices through guises, optical illusions, symbols, lexicon, and messaging that would not be detected as overtly threatening to the sensibilities of the oppressor. The rites of passage "way" conveyed through my Divine assignment took on a different expression based on the ecosystem and social conditions that it was created within, yet served as a healing modality and liberation tool that transformed the lives of thousands of boys and young men of African, Aboriginal, and Indigenous ancestry. It is only through the rearview mirror that I can now recognize that the rite of passage experiences that have lived in my mission and practices were healing modalities that have increasingly become more potent with each experience providing more practical tools and methods to be shared.

Spirit and my Ancestors have guided me to carry the rites of passage practice to many communities under many different names. The most recent expression of my Divine purpose is now experienced through Akoben Enterprise and the Mahaba House. Both initiations are intentional about using Indigenous Spiritual Technology, engaged healing centered practices, radical rituals, and elemental immersion initiations inspired by the Dagara people of Burkina Faso under the Spiritual Ambassadorship of the late Malidoma Somé. As this mission evolves and expands, there will still be a place for the facilitation of rites of passage in the conventional institutions where our children are often miseducated and receive limited access to experiences that help them to cultivate their geniuses, activate identity and dormant gifts to actualize Divine purpose driven lives.

The initiation rites processes are pervasive experiences that are a part of the only constant in the world, change. As I bring closure to the initiation of authoring this book, I recognize that I am not the same man that I was when I embarked on this writing journey. I experienced every phase of the initiatory rites process when producing this book and though I have knowledge and experiences of how this transformational progression works, I did not escape the mental, emotional, Spiritual, and at times physical turmoil that each phase of an initiation presents. As I reflect on who I am as I conclude this book, I have metaphorically died to some of the concepts, beliefs and principles that once defined me at certain phases of my life. I affirm that I am a vehicle for healing and enlightenment on the planet through various modalities of restoration. In this iteration of my journey, I am present as an educator, consultant, speaker, coach, counselor, ritualist, drummer, entrepreneur, *Jegna*, brother, husband, father, son, friend, facilitator, administrator, ceremonial leader, cultural custodian, keeper of sacred space, and a blossoming elder. Now I will sometimes appear as a writer (powered by Tehuti) who will use this mode of expression to convey the constant and predominate messages that have been consistently expressed through me: an ancient voice that carries transformative and healing energy through Indigenous and modern technology here to restore humanity back to Indigenous ways of thinking, knowing and being.

As I reincorporate back into life as an author, I look forward to continuing to grow, expand, and share the lessons of what this sacred educational and socialization method (initiation rites) continues to teach and inspire in me. My intention is to contribute to the elevation and expansion of Spiritual consciousness through reconnecting my community to their Indigenous intelligences and sensibilities.

As you continue to engage in your own elevation, expansion, and transformation, you are now equipped to locate where you are in your initiation path. As no one escapes the discomfort and dissonance that growth and change bring, you will at least know where you are in the cycle of your evolution. Additionally, as you have become aware of the significant formal and informal initiations that you have experienced, you are now poised to take a bold step into planning an initiation for your family and community. In launching anything, we never think or feel that we are fully equipped. As you embark on this path of facilitation, know that deeper learning comes through intentional engagement and the trials that will emerge. In *Crossing the Threshold*, you have been given some fundamentals that can move you from thought to action. It is time to take the leap into the experience and trust that you will attract the right facilitators (*Jegnas*), abundant resources, and tools essential to curating your own initiation rite experiences.

I am proud of you for embracing your call! I am excited to know that more communities will benefit from the rites of passage practice and contribute to helping all members of our communities identify, claim, and live according to the Divine design of their lives by sharing their powerful gifts and medicines with the world. **Your role as a rites of passage facilitator is needed more than ever to support the becoming process for our boys and young men.** I trust that through this powerful practice we will find our collective mission and cultivate the minds and spirits that will transform the world! *Ashe*!

VISION QUEST

3 Days and 2 Nights

Pre-Activity Guided questions and Severance exercises:

The initiate will need to begin to study and prepare for the fast and the general tenets of the Vision Quest protocols. Vision Quest allows initiates to gain access to themselves. They can experience themselves as they are when nobody else sees them, as they are when they are hungry and afraid.

In establishing the right mindset for the journey, the following are some assignments that are essential prior to embarking on this initiation.

➤ How can you prove that you are ready to leave your mother, father, and the childhood security of home to face the future as an adult?

➤ Create a farewell letter to the child you are leaving behind upon departing for your journey. The letter should be written in the spirit of love and gratitude for all the lessons learned. Also, be specific about the childhood memories, mindset, and behaviors that you are leaving behind as you prepare for your journey.

➤ Prepare a statement for family and friends that expresses your intentions for the journey, how they can support you and what expectations that you have of them upon your return.

➤ Preparation for Ceremony – As you create the itinerary, include family members, teachers, *Jegnas*, and advisors who have demonstrated a commitment to your spiritual growth. The following guide will help with creating what the rituals and trials will be during your Vision Quest:

1. What is the main reason that I desire to participate in this initiation?

    a. Is it a SEVERANCE? (A saying a goodbye, a letting go of, a termination, a parting, a separation)

    b. Is it a THRESHOLD? (A transition, a change in significant behavior, an adjustment, a shift in role, a new career, a move, a personal transformation)

    c. Is it a RETURN? (Taking on civilization again, coming together, a re-establishing of harmony, a joining after a separation, a taking on a new responsibility, a reaffirmation)

2. What "symbolic actions" would express (mark) my intent most meaningfully?

    Examples of "symbolic actions": burying, burning, smashing, name change, bathing, using masks, making vows, drawing blood, cutting hair, heaping stones, creating sacred space, creating an altar, pouring libations, elemental rituals, chanting, rattling, dancing, singing, tying knots, untying knots, lighting candles or a fire, going nude, making offerings, giving gifts, using incense, praying, meditating, kneeling, etc.

3. What symbols or objects do I want to use? This entails a review of your personal life and the objects or symbols that have power and meaning to you.

4. What if anything do I want to say during my ceremony - and to whom?

5. In what order do I want to do all the things that I plan to do?

6. Do I want anyone else there (in spirit or in person)? Do I want witnesses?

7. Where do I want to perform this ceremony and when? (Little, p. 92)

Be sure to consult with *Jegnas* and other custodians of rites practices as they can help you customize and choreograph an initiation and ceremony that aligns with your core values and belief system, as well as the community's ethos and practices. Also, they will be able to ensure that you are taking all the necessary precautions to be safe.

Trials (Crossing the Threshold)/Exercises:

The following are some recommended rituals and trials during your Vision Quest:

Invocations/Prayers/Libations
Creating an Ancestral Altar
Meditation/Tai Chi/Chi Gong
Calisthenics
Water Ritual
Earth Ritual
Fire Ritual
Medicine Walk
Earthing
Star Gazing
Musical Expressions (Acoustic Instruments/Songs)
Dance

The Return: Post Journey Trials for Reincorporation

In a ritualistic manner, the initiate will take in the scenery one last time before being welcomed back into the secular world. This is the time when the initiate will leave one last artifact that reflects something that he does not want to bring back into the next stage of his journey. Also, before embarking back on his journey home, he should leave another offering to the elements that cared for him during his encampment.

Bringing the Vision to Earth Presentation

Upon the initiate's return to family, friends and the *Jegnas*, he will be received, celebrated, and present his vision. The following are guided questions that can support his sharing:

> Describe what you experienced during your Vision Quest? (Visions, emotions, revelations, symbols, lessons, enlightenment, Spirit Guides, Ancestors, trauma, pain teachers, ego death, fears, confusion, stagnation, celebrations, etc.).

> Describe the challenges that you encountered during your quest.

> What did your quest reveal to you about your life? purpose? gifts? pain? shadows/dark narratives? fears? patterns? dormant attributes? Ancestral messages? Indigenous wisdom or practices?

> How do you plan to integrate and apply the lessons learned through your quest? What action steps will you take (have you taken) to apply the information and inspiration that you received?

> What questions and wonderings have emerged upon your journey?

> How have you grown or become more whole upon your Vision Quest?

> What dormant powers, intelligences and sensibilities were revealed to you about yourself?

> What did the quest reveal that you still don't comprehend and will have to continue to grow to *overstand*?

> What is the plan to make the necessary life changes that bring peace, wellness, joy, abundance, and support for your highest truth?

➤ How did the quest help you address old thought patterns, programming, conditioning, and belief systems that no longer serve you?

➤ Would you recommend the quest for peers interested in living from their most authentic self? Describe the value and benefits of Vision Quest?

➤ What vision will you now manifest? How will you deploy your purpose and gifts? What support will you need to execute your vision?

Sometimes the initiate will present gifts that were received from nature. The gifts can be songs, poems, or special words that were inspired during the quest. Some initiates bring back rocks, branches, or something that they created from nature, to which they have assigned a special meaning and which reflects their thoughts, emotions, or Spiritual insights. These gifts can be offered directly to a person or as a collective. However the initiate conceives the sharing, there should be a personal ritual of giving during the ceremony for it is dangerous to receive illumination without channeling it to others. The intention for this ritual is the willingness to be a medium, to offer the sacredness of his quest to those who held space for him from a distance through prayers, meditation, and loving thoughts.

After the share, the community will enjoy a simple meal together. Keep in mind to not overindulge as the initiate's "eyes will be larger than his stomach "as a response to his fast. In other words, be mindful that the initiate doesn't' have a gluttonous binge and that he eats moderately, as eating too much could have negative consequences.

Before the initiate re-enters the world, it will be of great significance for him to wash away the "dust of the sacred world." By symbolically washing the entire body, the initiate signifies his resolution to return and not meander in the threshold world. The ceremony is solidified and enhanced by the changing of clothes (Little, p. 104).

SEAT OF MA'AT

Developed by Kamau Ptah, Harambee Rites of Passage Group, Inc. (1995); revised by Kamau Ptah, Urban Assembly Academy of History and Citizenship for Young Men (2005); revised by Kamau Ptah, Sankofa Passages Program (2010).

Purpose

Ma'at is a sacred system of ethics that has its origins in the Nile Valley Civilizations of antiquity. It represents the moral ideal that citizens of Kemet (Known today as Egypt) and other nation states of the Nile Valley strived to uphold as individuals and a society. The virtues of Ma'at are Truth, Justice, Harmony, Reciprocity, Balance, Order and Righteousness. Ma'at is always seen with an ostrich feather headdress. In ancient Kemetic cosmogony it was believed that when a person dies their heart is weighed against the feather of Ma'at to assess the goodness of their life. This weighing on the scales of justice was a ritual for determining if a newly deceased person would be permitted to enter the Afterlife. Only those individuals whose hearts were lighter than Ma'at's feather were permitted to pass through into immortality with the Divine.

The Seat of Ma'at was designed for an individual (initiate) who is at the crossroads of her/his life and needs to examine her/his core truths, value system and current life circumstances that are impeding them from actualizing their life's purpose or calling. This process is also used when an individual is about to enter a new phase of their life and needs to rid themselves of old attitudes, toxic emotions, and undesirable behaviors that they no longer want to carry with them in their next chapter of life. This symbolic death will "lighten the load" that guilt, fear, anger, or any other painful and traumatic experience may have on stymying the evolution of one's Spiritual, mental, emotional, and moral development.

A loving community serves as guides prepared to listen attentively, ask critical and clarifying questions, affirm identity, challenge thought and behavioral patterns and sympathetically charge their sister/brother with some action steps that will help them move in a direction that aligns with their mission, goals, values, and core truths.

Time:

60-120 minutes

Roles:

Facilitator: The Seat of Ma'at Lead *Jegna* should be highly respected in the community and must have demonstrated that they have internalized and continue to strive to live the mission and virtues of their community.

The Lead *Jegna* makes the call and establishes the rationale, benefits, and instructions for the trial.

Participants:

A group, size ranging from 5-15 people (it's ideal to have a wide range of adult aged members from younger adults to elders) is invited to participate by the Seat of Ma'at initiate (in some cases the initiate does not choose). Whatever the scenario, the initiate must feel completely comfortable with some of the group members that will participate in the ritual. The initiate also chooses who he would like to facilitate the process. The group members are people that inspire trust or are part of a community that has demonstrated a commitment to living the virtues and codes of conduct of the organization (group).

Process:

The Ma'at facilitator helps to establish the sacred ambiance for the ritual. She/He gives a brief explanation of Ma'at (see above), discusses the intent and protocols for the optimal outcomes of the session and guides the procedures with clarity. The following are some of the prompts that will help the facilitator get started upon the overview and procedures:

1. With the name of Force/Virtues/Legacy that the group upholds (as articulated in your institution or organization's mission and governing values) …we are assembled here today for Brother/ Sister (ADD NAME)_____Seat of Ma'at Ritual/ Protocol. Give initiate an ostrich feather to hold as a symbol that represents the weighing of his heart.

2. The norms and guidelines for the optimal outcomes of our session are to:

   a. Listen attentively to the initiate's statements, responses to questions, and take notes (mental and physical)

   b. Ask heartfelt integrity questions when the time is allotted.

   c. Respond to questions directed to you by the initiate.

   d. Provide constructive critical feedback when time is allotted.

   e. Provide affirmative and empowering feedback when time is allotted.

   f. Listen attentively to the final statement that is made by the initiate.

   g. Respond to the call from the facilitator when he states, "Think Ma'at; Speak Ma'at; Do Ma'at."

Opening Questions (asked by the facilitator):

1. What Divine Force(s) and Ancestral powers do you want present with you on your Seat of Ma'at journey? Explain why.

2. What heart truths are you prepared to examine today?

3. At this phase of your journey, what is your heart yearning to know and express?

4. What experiences have created heartfelt joy in your life? What makes your heart sing?

5. Name a person or people who have created the most pain in your heart. What would it take for you to begin forgiving them?

6. What heartaches or traumas are you prepared to release today?

7. Where is your heart at this moment?

8. What are heartfelt adjectives or terms that describe your authentic self?

9. As I envision my heart at its optimal health, I take time to care for my heart by...

10. Describe your Divine purpose.

11. What evidence do you have that reflects that you are living your purpose?

12. Describe the obstacles that are preventing you from realizing your purpose...

13. What must you become to live your purpose? What attributes do you possess that are in alignment with your purpose? What must be let go to truly be in integrity with your purpose? What support do you need to achieve your purpose?

Questions asked by the collective:

Once the initiate answers at least half of the questions, the collective begins to ask their questions. These inquiries come from personal knowledge of the initiate's life journey. The questions don't have to follow the logic of the other questions. The questions that first come to mind are the questions that should be asked. If the initiate's body language or eyes trigger questions, those are the queries that should be presented. Each member can ask one question. If time permits, additional questions can be asked.

The initiate responds to the questions with heartfelt truths. If an initiate finds any of the questions too invasive or does not feel comfortable responding to the question, she/he may pass. The only questions that the initiate asks during this segment are clarifying questions.

Respond to questions asked by the initiate:

During this segment, the initiate can ask general or specific questions to the members of the community. If the initiate requests feedback from a particular community member, he may address that question specifically to the person he desires a response from.

Constructive Critical feedback:

At this phase of the ritual/protocol, each member will have an opportunity to offer constructive and critical feedback. This feedback will focus on where we know the initiate is vulnerable. The advice is constructive as it looks at the vulnerable areas as an opportunity to strengthen and evolve to the next phase of development.

Affirmative and empowering feedback:

At this phase of the ritual/protocol, the members of the community provide affirmative and empowering feedback that helps guide the initiate's actions towards his vision. The community members acknowledge the powerful attributes of the initiate and speak to his potential for overcoming her/his challenge and fulfilling her/his mission.

Initiates' Final Statement:

During this final phase, the initiate reflects on the key issues or themes that came up during the ritual. She/He identifies lessons and strategies (action steps) that will be implemented moving forward. She/He seeks support in areas that will be difficult moving forward. The initiate reflects on the Seat of Ma'at process and discusses the benefits and challenges of the ritual.

Call and Response:

The facilitator closes the session out by leading the following call and response:

"Think Ma'at!
Speak Ma'at!!
Do Ma'at!!!"
Ashe', Ashe', Ashéoooo!!!!!

EYE OF HERU

Heru is an ancient Kemetic Divine force of nature represented as a falcon's eye. Falcons are known for their keen sight, speed, and their ability to fly high in the sky. Also, falcons can look directly into the sun without harming their eyes. The Eye of Heru represents awareness and protection from negativity.

The Eye of Heru ritual involves making direct eye contact with a brother, while reflecting on questions centered on identity, purpose, vulnerabilities, and infinite possibilities. The trial strengthens intuitive sensibilities, communication, self-worth, and vision. Additionally, the Eye of Heru builds brotherhood bonds and invites initiates to use their intuitive intelligences to convey Spirit inspired messages.

Time: 60-90 minutes

Roles: Lead *Jegna*: The Eye of Heru Lead *Jegna* should be highly respected in the community and must have demonstrated that they have internalized and continue to strive to live the mission and virtues of their community.

The Lead *Jegna* makes the call and establishes the rationale, benefits, and instructions for the trial.

Number of Participants: 30-40 initiates

Process:

1. The Lead *Jegna* will instruct everyone to create an inner and outer circle.

2. The Lead *Jegna* will instruct everyone to make eye contact with the person standing in front of them. He will invite everyone to participate in the "call and response" statement that asserts, "the Divine Warrior in me recognizes the Divine Warrior in you." After the statement is made the initiates will maintain eye contact for one minute. As the initiates are looking intently into each other's eyes, the Lead *Jegna* will ask the first question (see below). The initiate from the inner circle will respond first, and upon the completion of time, the initiate from the outer circle will respond. Each initiate will have 2 minutes to respond to the question.

3. The Lead *Jegna* will instruct the initiates from the inner circle to move to their right and introduce themselves (if they don't know each other) to their new partner. If they know each other, perform the brotherhood handshake learned through the rites of passage or create one for the trial. He will have the initiates repeat step 2 and guide them through the second question.

4. The Lead *Jegna* will guide this concentric* circle process until the last question. It is not a problem if everyone doesn't get to share with all participants. Each initiate should have at least 4-5 opportunities to engage with another brother during the Eye of Heru trial.

Questions:

1. What positive qualities does this brother possess?

2. What is this brother's Spirit communicating in this moment?

3. What do you think or feel is this brother's greatest Superpower(s)?

4. What do you see in this brother that he may not see in himself?

5. What challenges do you sense that the brother may be presently experiencing in life?

6. How does this brother's energy make you feel?

7. How will this brother's energy contribute to improving his family, community, and world?

8. What do you think or feel this brother is willing to sacrifice, live and die for?

9. What do you think or feel are the biggest obstacles confronting this brother?

10. What do you think is the highest vision for this brother's life?

11. How can this brother contribute to your life and mission? How can you contribute to his life and mission?

12. What are the greatest lessons that this brother has learned up to this point in his life?

Sankofa Reflection of The Eye of Heru:

1. What surfaced for you as you participated in this trial?

2. How did it feel to look at your brother and have him read into your personal narrative?

3. What did brothers say about you that was accurate and insightful?

4. What did you learn about yourself during this exercise?

5. What did you learn about others during this trial?

6. How can this experience benefit the way that you view yourself and the daily decisions that you make?

7. What areas of your life do you feel you need to pay more attention to, particularly the areas where you feel most vulnerable?

8. What thoughts, ideas, and perceptions of yourself were reinforced during the Eye of Heru trial?

9. What did another brother do or say that made you feel comfortable? Uncomfortable? What can you take away from these impressions?

10. Was anything that you heard surprising or new to you?

11. Were there any questions that were particularly difficult for you to answer? Explain …

12. What questions did you enjoy answering?

13. Offer a Warrior Acknowledgement to a brother who you felt a strong connection to or who shared something that enlightened or encouraged you to view something in a different manner.

* In this ritual, the initiates stand in two concentric circles, i.e., circles with a common center but different radii. They face one another and respond to a question in a paired discussion. When prompted by the Lead Jegna, one of the circles moves to the left or right so each initiate now faces a new partner, with whom they discuss a new question.

PROMISE LAND TRIAL

In the quest for freedom, people of African Ancestry used this "Promise Land" passage and Gospel Hymn references to interpret their collective plight as people who were in bondage under the cruel system of slavery. The "Promised Land "in the enslaved African imagination, lived up to being an egalitarian utopia for fugitives in many ways. In Canada, slavery was denounced in 1793 and was formally abolished in 1834. Many enslaved Africans put their lives on the line and escaped the plantation to journey north in quest for freedom, if necessary, even to Canada.

The Promised Land Trial takes place in a remote forest area where the initiates experience a simulated Underground Railroad route to freedom. At each Underground Railroad station, the initiates are asked questions by *Jegnas* about information that they should have mastered during their initiation. If answered correctly, the Guides of the Underground Railroad share clues on how to get to the next Underground Railroad station. The initiates must be watchful of the simulated slave catchers that search the trails for runaways.

Time: 2-4 Hours

Number of Participants: 40-50 Initiates, 4-5 *Jegnas*, 2-3 Volunteers

Setting: Wooded area/Retreat Location/State Park

Roles:

Lead *Jegna*

> ➤ Establishes the call for the trial.

> ➤ Opens with ritual (Invocation, Libation and Call and Responses)

> ➤ Instructs *Jegnas* on their role as slave catchers.

> ➤ Choreographs the beginning of the "separation" of the trial, where initiates are left alone to problem solve.

Jegnas:

Jegnas will simulate the role of slave catchers and attempt to catch the initiates as they attempt to escape to "The Promised Land."

Underground Railroad Conductors (At least 3, no more than 5 *Jegnas* and volunteer chaperones):

The conductors are stationed in the wooded area and support the initiates by providing clues to the Promise Land. For the initiates to receive clues for their next destination they must answer questions and know essential information that relates to their entire rites of passage experiences to date. Also, they must work in unity to answer questions and solve problems before being given hints and strategies for their next destination.

The Lead *Jegna* or an assigned *Jegna* maintains his role and observes the trial with the intention of ensuring safety for all initiates and *Jegnas*.

Process:

To set the stage, the Lead *Jegna* will open with the call and an overview of the "Promised Land" concept. He will not contextualize the Promised Land with the trial that the young men will participate in as that will occur as a surprise. He will perform a powerful ritual that inspires courage and a Warrior's Spirit!

Upon the completion of the ritual, the initiates will be blindfolded and guided to an area that they have not explored and is far from where they began. During the walk, the *Jegnas* will be guiding the initiates through obstacles that are disorienting and fear inducing. They will be reciting positive affirmations and sharing words of encouragement during the entire journey. Once the group reaches their destination, the *Jegnas* and volunteers will head to their designated stations in the woods with their instruments and sound tools and prepare for the initiates to embark on their Promised Land journey. An experienced *Jegna*, not the Lead *Jegna*, will remain with the initiates and place them in groups. Once everyone is assigned a group, he will instruct them to take off their blindfolds and begin to contextualize the trial. Here's the following summation of the narrative he will share:

"You have just taken a Sankofa Journey back in time. You are now an enslaved African on the plantation in the south. You and your brothers have decided that enough is enough and you have planned your escape to freedom. Currently the slave catchers are aware of your escape and are on the hound to return you back to your plantation. I advise you to stay vigilante and alert throughout this entire journey as one wrong move will cost you your opportunity to be free. You have come so far and have just a few miles to go before reaching the Promised Land, where opportunities to experience a greater quality of life exist. Listen to me with more than your ears. Listen to the following instructions with your entire being, as the information I share will put you on the path to the Underground Railroad where you will receive vital information and support on your freedom journey":

1. Do you hear the various sounds? Those are the Underground Railroad locations. The stations are in the woods off the main road. With your group follow the sounds and a conductor will be there to provide you with more information if you are able to respond to certain questions and demonstrate unity as a collective.

2. Be aware of the slave catchers, particularly as you travel the main roads.

3. Your success will be determined by how well you strategize and work as a unified collective.

4. Listen intently to the Underground Railroad conductors. They will give you directions to your next destination.

5. Be careful in the wooded areas. Be sure that you don't run into a ditch or a tree.

6. If you are feeling overwhelmed by the experience and need to disengage with the experience, have your group shout out, *"HARAMBEE."*

Upon completion of the trial, gather everyone in the group to process the experience. The following are some guiding questions to explore:

1. Did you make it to the Promised Land with your entire group? Explain

2. What were your thoughts and feelings about this trial? What resonates with you about this experience?

3. How did your group work as a collective? What were the areas of strength? What were the challenges?

4. What does freedom mean to you? Are you free? Explain

5. What freedoms do you take for granted?

6. What are your thoughts about the Ancestors who chose to escape plantations and seek freedom? Do you think that you would have taken the risk and run away? Explain

7. What areas of your life are you enslaved to (unproductive thoughts, habits, self-imposed limitations, mental and emotional attachments, technology attachment/addiction, undesirable patterns, insecurities, doubts, fears, pain memories)?

8. Describe what restricts and threatens your freedom? How do you protect your freedom?

9. What is your freedom plan?

10. As a free young man, describe who you are. What do you do with your freedom?

11. Who do you know that enjoys the freedom that you desire? Give examples of what represents freedom from your perspective?

APPENDIX 5

Elemental Immersion Initiation:

Inspired by Dagara Indigenous Spiritual Technology, initiates experience sacred rituals designed to release, restore, reconnect, and affirm a purpose-driven life. Through Earth, Fire, Water, Nature, and Mineral rituals, this Elemental Immersion initiation guides aspirants to the infinite wisdom of the elemental teachers who support in the remembrance of our gifts and purpose and help to clear internal impediments that block us from actualizing the Divine assignment that we are here to express.

Earth Ritual Rationale:

According to Malidoma Patrice Somé, "Earth rituals greatly emphasize the sense of belonging, self-worth, and community, including all forms of relationships." The earth is our place of origin, and her elements are a part of human physical make-up. Earth represents survival and healing, unconditional love and caring. Earth loves to give and gives love abundantly." Earth rituals are facilitated as a return to our home. Mother earth is the great connector and provides provisions unconditionally. The earth helps to alleviate feelings of detachment, isolation, anonymity, and purposelessness, which are symptoms of being disconnected from the earth.

Time: 2-3Hours

Number of Participants: 20-25 Initiates and 4-5 *Jegnas*

Setting: Back Yard/Wooded area/Retreat Location/State Park

Preferably facilitated at night

Roles: Lead *Jegna* and *Jegnas* will establish the appropriate ambience for the trial by sharing the rationale for the ritual and the intelligences of the earth, particularly in a sacred ritual context. The Lead *Jegna* will open with the invocation to the Creator, the Spirit of the Earth, the Spirit of all the other elements (air, water, fire, mineral and nature), and the Ancestors.

Jegnas will serve as *gatekeepers* and "hold space" during the trial/ritual. They will ensure that the initiates are safe, and the proper *containers* are present to maintain high intentions and continuity during the experience.

Musicians will play during the ritual and establish the appropriate atmosphere for the transformation (Metaphoric death and declarations)

Lead *Jegnas*:

➤ Establish the call for the trial.

➤ Provide instructions for the pre-ritual trial.

➤ Open with ritual (Invocation must include the summoning of the Earth's Spirit, Libation, Offerings, and Call and Responses).

➤ Co-facilitates the reflection and processing of the trial/ritual.

Process:

Jegnas will present the following instructions to the initiates for the pre-trial activity:

1. Dig small holes into the earth (approximately ten inches deep and ten inches wide). Dig five holes for twenty-five initiates to engage in the trial/ritual.

2. Make an offering into the earth (coffee beans, sage, corn meal, flowers, honey, pennies, etc.)

3. Set intentions for what you desire to receive upon the completion of this ritual.

4. With sticks, rocks, and candles, create a demarcation between the ritual space and the village location. Make sure that there is a pathway that leads to the entrance of the ritual space.

The Ritual Will Consist of:

1. A drum call to alert everyone that the ritual is about to begin and to set the appropriate atmosphere for the trial/ritual. The drums will be played during the entire trial/ritual. The rhythm will be the container for the ritual.

2. The Lead *Jegna's* invocation and libation.

3. The gatekeepers will welcome each initiate at the pathway to the ritual space. They will thoroughly explain the ritual and help the initiate enter the experience with the right mindset.

4. The *Jegna* will line the initiates up to each hole (5 per hole)

5. The initiates will be instructed to lie on their stomachs and place their face over the hole and release all thoughts and emotions that no longer serve them in life and make declarations about what their hearts truly desire. They will bring their deepest issues and challenges and speak to them into the hole and release them into the earth.

6. After each initiate completes the ritual, one of the *Jegnas* will sage the hole in preparation for the next initiate.

7. Upon completion of the earth ritual, initiates will return to the designated location that serves as a village, where they will be welcomed with joyful and celebratory cheers, applause, and acknowledgement.

8. After everyone returns to the village, the drumming and dancing will come to an ecstatic climax and completion.

9. Lastly, the initiates will collectively reflect on the trial/ritual through an integration process.

The following are some reflective questions for the Earth Ritual:

1. Describe the thoughts and emotions that came up for you during the Earth Ritual.

2. What was challenging about the trial/ritual? What message did Mother Earth share with you?

3. How do you feel now that the earth has absorbed and alchemized your purging to support your highest intentions?

4. If you feel comfortable sharing, what did you declare and how will you integrate the enlightenment received from this trial/ritual?

Fire Ritual

Fire Rationale: In the Dagara cosmogony, the fire ritual is the Indigenous belief that each person is born with a purpose, and that this purpose was presented to the council of the ancestors in the Spirit World for approval prior to each person's journey to Earth. With that Spiritual framework, the fire ritual represents a call to identify, claim and live one's Divine purpose. Fire represents the portal to the ancestral world and devours blockages to manifesting purpose. Malidoma Somé asserts, "In order to fulfill our purpose, we need the driving force of fire, just as a vehicle needs fuel to reach its destination" (Somé, p. 210)

Time: 3 Hours

Number of Participants: 20-25

Setting: Back Yard/Wooded area/Retreat Location/State Park
Preferably facilitated at night

Roles: Lead *Jegna* and *Jegnas* will establish the appropriate ambience for the trial by sharing the rationale for the ritual and the intelligences of the earth, particularly in a sacred ritual context. The Lead *Jegna* will open with the invocation to the Creator, the Spirit of the Earth, the Spirit of all the other elements (air, water, fire, mineral and nature), and the Ancestors.

Jegnas will serve as *gatekeepers* and "hold space" during the trial/ritual. They will ensure that the initiates are safe, and the proper *containers* are present to maintain high intentions and continuity during the experience.

Musicians will play during the ritual and establish the appropriate atmosphere for the transformation (Metaphoric death and declarations)

Lead *Jegnas*:

➤ Establish the call for the trial.

➤ Provide instructions for the pre-ritual trial.

➤ Open with ritual (Invocation must include the summoning of the Fire's Spirit, Libation, Offerings, and Call and Responses).

➤ Co-facilitate the reflection and processing of the trial/ritual.

Process:

Jegnas will present the following instructions to the initiates for the pre-trial activity:

1. Collectively gather large pieces of wood, small twigs, sticks, dry leaves, grass, and needles.

2. Initiates will make an offering into the firepit (coffee beans, sage, corn meal, flowers, pennies, etc.)

3. With sticks, rocks, and candles, initiates collectively create a demarcation between the ritual space and the village location.

Make sure that there is a distinct pathway that leads to the entrance of the ritual space.

4. Initiates will gather tree branches, flowers, acorns, pinecones, grass, etc. They will place items in a paper that has their greatest desires that they would like to attract and the issues, challenges, barriers that are impediments to living their purpose and greatest self-expression. They will tie their items wrapped in the paper into a bundle, which will be placed in the fire during the trial/ritual.

The Ritual Will Consist of:

1. A drum call to alert everyone that the ritual is about to begin and to set the appropriate atmosphere for the trial/ritual. The drums will be played during the entire trial/ritual. The rhythm will be the container for the ritual.

2. The Lead *Jegna's* invocation and libation.

3. The gatekeepers will welcome each initiate at the pathway to the ritual space. They will thoroughly explain the fire ritual and help the initiate enter the experience with the right mindset.

4. The *Jegnas* will line the initiates up to the entry of the firepit.

5. The initiates will be instructed to release their bundles containing all thoughts and emotions that no longer serve them in life and make declarations about what their hearts truly desire. They will bring their deepest issues and challenges that reflect impediments to living their Divine purpose and release them into fire.

6. Upon completion of the fire ritual, initiates will return to the designated location that serves as a village, where they will be welcomed with joyful and celebratory cheers, applause, and acknowledgement.

7. After everyone returns to the village the drumming and dancing will come to an ecstatic climax and completion.

8. Lastly, the initiates will collectively reflect on the trial/ritual through an integration process.

The following are some reflective questions for the Fire Ritual:

1. Describe the thoughts and emotions that came up for you during the Fire Ritual.

2. What was challenging about the trial/ritual? What message did the fire share with you?

3. How do you feel now that the fire has absorbed and alchemized your purging to support your highest intentions?

4. If you feel comfortable sharing, what did you declare and how will you integrate the enlightenment received from this trial/ritual?

Water Ritual

Rationale: Water is symbolic of cleansing, purification, reconciliation, healing, and establishing harmony in the face of life's trials. Water rituals help to shed the massive accumulation of negative emotion due to loss, failure, and powerlessness. Also, as water is recognized as the source of life, water rituals are essential to giving birth to new ways of knowing and being.

Time: 3 Hours

Number of Participants: 30-40

Setting: Camp Lake, Beach, Waterfall, Ocean

Roles: Lead *Jegna* and *Jegnas* will establish the appropriate ambience for the trial by sharing the rationale for the ritual and the intelligences of the water, particularly in a sacred ritual context. The Lead *Jegna* will open with invocations to the Creator, the Spirit of the Water, the Spirit of all the other elements (air, fire, mineral and nature), and the

Ancestors (Including the Ancestors who reside in the Middle Passage Atlantic Ocean).

Jegnas will serve as *gatekeepers* and "hold space" during the trial/ritual. They will ensure that the initiates are safe, and the proper *containers* are present to maintain high intentions and continuity during the experience.

Musicians will play during the ritual and establish the appropriate atmosphere for the transformation (Metaphoric death and declarations)

Lead *Jegnas*:

➢ Establish the call for the trial.

➢ Provide instructions for the pre-ritual trial.

➢ Open with ritual (Invocation must include the summoning of the Water's Spirit, Libation, Offerings to the water and Call and Responses).

➢ Co-facilitate the reflection and processing of the trial/ritual.

Process:

Jegnas will present the following instructions to the initiates for the pre-trial activity:

1. Initiates will walk in a line (from eldest to the youngest) to the water while singing songs and participating in call and responses.

2. Initiates will make an offering into the water (coffee beans, red kola nut, sage, honey, corn meal, corn kernels, rum, flowers, pennies, etc.)

3. With sticks, rocks, and candles, initiates collectively create a demarcation between the ritual space and the village location. Make sure there is a distinct pathway that leads to the entrance of the ritual space.

The Ritual Will Consist of:

1. A drum call to alert everyone that the ritual is about to begin and to set the appropriate atmosphere for the trial/ritual. The drums and other acoustic instruments will be played during the entire trial/ritual. The rhythm will be the container for the ritual.

2. The Lead *Jegna's* invocation and libation. Communicate to the Spirit of the Water that our collective intention is to have the Spirit of the Water remove all barriers and forces of adversity that are standing in the way of delivering our gifts collectively. Also, request the Ancestor's guidance, particularly the Ancestors whose remains are on the ocean floors of the Atlantic.

3. The gatekeepers will welcome each initiate at the pathway to the ritual space. They will thoroughly explain the water ritual and help the initiate enter the experience with the right mindset.

4. The *Jegnas* will line the initiates up to the entry of the pathway to the water.

5. The initiates will be instructed to enter the water where there will be two *Jegnas* who are assigned to welcome them and immerse them under the water. The initiates will be charged to stay under the water as long as they can and invite the Water Spirit to enter and cleanse them completely. This process will be repeated at least four times in a row before exiting the water. The initiate will lie face down and the *Jegnas* will hold them until they are prepared to come up for air.

6. Upon completion of the water ritual, initiates will return to the designated location that serves as a village, where they will be welcomed with joyful and celebratory cheers, applause, and acknowledgement.

7. After everyone returns to the village the music and dancing will end.

8. Lastly, the initiates will collectively reflect on the trial/ritual through an integration process.

The Following are Some Reflective Questions for the Water Ritual:

1. Describe the thoughts and emotions that came up for you during the Water Ritual.

2. What was challenging about the trial/ritual? What message did the water share with you?

3. How do you feel now that the water has cleansed and purified you and birthed new insights and sensibilities?

4. How will you carry the wisdom of the water with you upon your reincorporation back into life?

Mineral Ritual

Rationale: Dagara wisdom teaches that minerals (stones, rocks, crystals, iron, etc.) are the storage place of memory, creativity, narratives, resources, and allegory/symbolism (Somé p. 177). Mineral rituals are designed to help return lost memories, particularly as they relate to the life purpose of human beings. The expression "I can feel it in my bones" is a reminder that there are intelligences and spiritual retentions that exist that are stored in the marrows of our bones.

Time: 1-2 Hours

Number of Participants: 25-30

Setting: Back yard/Wooded area/Retreat location/State Park/Indoor space that has been prepared for ritual and designated as sacred.

Roles: Lead *Jegna, Jegnas,* and Initiates will participate in narrative sharing and glean significant messages as they relate to our Sankofa Reflections (Retrieving past stories, bringing them to the present moment as we imagine and affirm our futures).

Process: During the integration and reflection process for all the rituals and trials, each initiate should have a crystal, stone, rock, or a mineral that will be held as they share distinct stages and phases of their lives.

The following are guiding Mineral inspired questions and prompts for sharing personal narratives and restoring memory:

1. Recall the moments of your life where you were engaged in experiences that made you feel a deep sense of connection and belonging.

2. Do you feel that you have a gift in this life? If so, would you be able to describe what your gift is?

3. Describe the moments where you are in the role of offering your gifts and purpose. What are you doing? How does it feel?

4. When in your life have you felt most challenged? What skills or mindset did you develop as a result?

5. Who am I really?

6. If this were the last day of my life, would I have the same plans for the day?

7. When do you feel most alive (on an inner level)?

8. What am I really scared of?

9. Am I holding on to something that I need to let go of?

10. What matters most in your life?

11. When was the last time that I pushed the boundaries of my comfort zone? Describe the moment.

12. What do I desire most in my life?

13. What am I doing about the things that matter most in my life?

14. What comes easy to you? What do you enjoy doing most?

15. Do you have an idea of what your life's purpose is? If so, what is it? Does your life purpose match with your daily activities in this moment? If not, ask someone who knows you well if they have an idea of what your purpose could be.

16. According to you, how do gifts and purpose relate to each other?

17. Are gifts and purpose interconnected in your life? If so, how do they relate to each other?

18. In your experience, is it sometimes difficult to be true to your gift and purpose? If so, what kind of obstacles have you faced? How did you deal with those obstacles?

19. What are you inclined to do when you feel like all kinds of obstacles are blocking you from living a gift and purpose driven life?

20. Reflect on how you have dealt with challenges in the past. How did you cope with those challenges? How did this impact (what you know to be) your gift and purpose?

21. When you look at people in your immediate surroundings, would you be able to describe what their gift and purpose is? What is the effect they have with their presence in your world?

22. What is the effect of your presence in the world on others? Would you be able to describe this? If not, you could ask someone.

23. What song, genre of music, movie, book, TV/Social Media personality, animal, artist, artifact, Ancestor, historical figure, quote(s), instrument(s), elements of nature (air, fire, earth, water), colors, shapes, natural sounds, plants, and/or seasonings captures best who you are as a Spirit having a human experience? Choose at least three and provide a detailed explanation.

24. Who are you at your highest self-expression?

25. What challenges have you overcome in life? What did these challenges teach you?

26. Respond to the following prompts:

27. When it comes to my Spiritual identity:
    - I think that I am...
    - I feel that I am...
    - I know that I am...

28. When it comes to my mental aptitude:
    ➤ I think that I am…
    ➤ I feel that I am…
    ➤ I know that I am…

29. When it comes to my emotional wellbeing:
    ➤ I think that I am…
    ➤ I feel that I am…
    ➤ I know that I am…

30. When it comes to my physical health:
    ➤ I think that I am…
    ➤ I feel that I am…
    ➤ I know that I am…

31. Where do you identify as your home? Describe what home means to you. When you think of home what thoughts and emotions come up for you?

32. What environments feel safe to you? Why?

33. Who makes you feel at home in this world? What people bring you a feeling of safety and comfort in this world?

34. When you think of legacy, what comes up for you?

35. If you were to transition (become an Ancestor) today, what accomplishments would you want people to remember? What would you want no one to remember? What would you be disappointed that you did not complete? Who do you think would take on your mission and pick up where you left off?

36. Design and write your own obituary.

37. If you had the power to orchestrate your birth, describe how you would like to be born?

38. What do I need to change about myself?

39. What do you love about life?

40. Describe your first love (person, place, or thing)

41. Make a list of everything that you would like to say yes to

42. Make a list of everything that you would like to say no to

43. I couldn't imagine life without...

44. The two moments I'll never forget in my life are...

45. Discuss ten things that make you smile.

Listening is essential to the storytelling process. This is why every mineral ritual must involve a period of listening, for listening is the complement of storytelling.

The listeners of the narratives should ask themselves:

➢ Where am I in the story?

➢ Who or what do I identify with?

➢ How does this narrative align with my life?

➢ What was shared that made me feel inspired? Explain

➢ What was shared that made me feel uncomfortable? Explain

➢ Why did I need to hear this narrative? What message(s) am I taking away from this story?

➢ What question(s) emerged for me when I heard this story?

➢ This narrative is inspiring me to act on...

BIBLIOGRAPHY

Afua, Queen. *Man Heal Thyself: Journey to Optimal Wellness*. Baltimore, MD: Afrikan World Books, 2012

Akbar, Na'im, PH.D. *Know Thyself.* Tallahassee, FL: Mind Production and Associates, 1998

Akbar, Na'im, PH.D. *Visions for Black Men.* Tallahassee, FL: Mind Productions and Associates, 1991

Akua, Chike, PH. D *Honoring Our Ancestral Obligations: 7 Steps to Black Student Success:* Imani Enterprises, 2015

Armah, Ayi K. *Two Thousand Seasons*. Popenguine, Senegal: Per Ankh 1973, 2000

Bolling, Bolling L. *The Heart of Soul: An Africentric Approach to Psycho-spiritual Wholeness*. New York, NY: Mandala Rising Press, 1990

Chernoff, J.L. *African Rhythm and African Sensibility: Aesthetics and Social Action in African Musical Idioms*. Chicago, IL: The University of Chicago Press, 1979

Diallo, Yaya and Hall, Mitchell. *The Healing Drum: African Wisdom Teachings*. Rochester, VT: Destiny Books, 1989

Foner, Eric. *Reconstruction – America's Unfinished Revolution 1863-1877.* Harper & Row, New York, NY 1988

Foor, Daniel, PH.D. *Ancestral Medicine: Rituals for Personal and Family Healing*. Rochester, VT: Bear & Company 2017

Karenga, Maulana, PH.D. Ma'at: *The Moral Ideal in Ancient Egypt.* Los Angeles, CA: University of Sankore Press 2006

Hare, Nathan, and Julia. *Bringing the Black Boy to Manhood.* San Francisco, CA: The Black Think Tank, 1985, 2nd Printing 2000.

Mahdi, Louise C., Foster, Steven, and Little, Meredith. *Betwixt and Between: Patterns of Masculine and Feminine Initiation.* LaSalle, IL: Open Court 1987

Millman, Dan. *Living on Purpose: Straight Answers to Life's Tough Questions.* Novato, CA: New World Library 2000

Somé Malidoma P. *The Healing Wisdom of Africa: Finding Life Purpose Through Nature, Ritual and Community*: New York, NY: Penguin Putnam Inc. 1998

Somé Malidoma P. *Ritual: Power, Healing and Community.* New York, NY: Penguin Putnam Inc. 1993

Tolle, Eckhart. *A New Earth: Awakening to Your Life's Purpose.* New York, NY: Penguin Group 2005

INDEX

GRATITUDE AND ACKNOWLEDGEMENT

Above all, I acknowledge the Creator, the Omnipotent, Omniscient, and Omnipresent Source of all Creation. I acknowledge my bloodline ancestors from the Patterson, Williams, Smalls, Jones, Taylor, Murray, Taylor, Burrowes, and Dolphy lineages for the powerful narratives that you have lived and the legacy that you have passed on to me for my journey. I acknowledge all my cultural ancestors of African, Indigenous, and Indian Ancestry for their devotion to the elevation and expansion of human consciousness, the Know Thyself path, liberation movements, creative expressions, and their example of purpose driven living imbued with love.

I pay loving homage to my father, Frank Patterson Jr. who now resides in the realm of the ancestors. Thank you for embracing the call to fatherhood. Your presence provided me with a curriculum for my manhood journey. I have internalized and continue to integrate all of what your light reflects and alchemize what the shadows have revealed. As you would often say, "the shadow knows."

I give thanks to my mother for enduring the pain of my birth and providing exposure to authentic cultural and artistic experiences that helped shape my identity. I am mostly grateful for our spiritual connection and the sacred bond that we share. I am thankful for my big brother, Dr. R.A. Ptahsen Shabazz. As my brother and friend, we have and continue to experience life passages (family, community, athletic, cultural, and spiritual) together. Also, I am grateful for your masterful editing of this book.

I acknowledge my wife, Nadhege for her deep love, passion, and ability to speak truth and create harmony, balance, and order in our family and all her spheres of influence. Thank you for always helping me raise the bar and never allowing me to settle for anything less than excellence in my life pursuits and passages. Thank you, Salim, Tsahai, and Tseday for initiating me as a Baba. You all bring me much love, joy, and pride in your daily pursuits of your emerging visions and missions.

After my baptism rite shortly after my birth, my first formal passages were academic, and athletic. I thank all the administrators, teachers, counselors, and staff who were a part of my education and miseducation passages in the Greenburgh Central 7 School District. Special acknowledgements to the following notable teachers: Mrs. Maggie Nelson (RIP), Ms. Newton (RIP), Ms. Pennyfeather, Mrs. Phyllis Brown, Mrs. Peggy Christian, Ms. Vilma France, Mrs. Barbara Glover, Ms. Maestro, Mr. Charles Deahl, Mrs. Golden, Ms. Mattie Sydnor, Mr. Dennis Avedon, Ms. Valentino, Mr. LaVigne, and Mr. Dan Smith.

I extend gratitude to the significant coaches during my athletic passages: Robert Smith and the Jaguar Track Club, John "Speedy" Austin and the Kenyan Runners Track Club, Brian Denman and the United States Youth Games team, Coach James Blakeny (RIP) and the East Side House Track Club. I thank my football coaches Mark Murray, Jimmy Red (RIP) and the entire Fairview Greenburgh Community Center (currently the Theodore D. Young Community Center-TDYCC) Golden Falcon's Football Team. Thank you to Coach Barkley and the players from the Mid-Westchester Warriors Football team. I offer gratitude and respect to all my basketball coaches and teammates. Coach Palladino and the Dad's Club Pacers, Coach Curtis "Bouncy" Thompson, Coach Jerry Glanville, and the Young Life basketball squad. All the coaches and teammates from Woodlands Middle and High School. I am thankful for my track coaches Carol Coram, Coach Watson, Coach John Miller, and Coach Joe Intervallo.

I thank all the cultural institutions, organizations, and Jegnas who supported my identity reclamation, formation and "Know Thyself" path. Acknowledgement to Bereshith Cultural Institution (Mount Vernon, NY) with distinguished Jegnas like Baba Abishai Ben Rueben, Rabbi Kohain Nathanyah Halevi, Priest Nasai Yahchain, and Brother Judah Williams (RIP). I thank the Association of Community Based Arts Center (AC-BAW) in Mount Vernon and its President Saleem Sullivan. I give thanks for the First World Alliance community and the cultural custodians of that institution (Kefa Nephthys (RIP), Bill Jones (RIP), and Yvonne Milliner (RIP). I thank Mfundishi Jhutyms Hassan Salim and the Kera Jhuty Heru Neb Hu community. I send gratitude to Mosque #7 in Harlem and the Fruit of Islam (FOI). Thank you, Dr. Khalid Abdul Muhammad (RIP), Abdul Hafeez Muhammad (RIP), Brother Jason X, Brother Elijah Shabazz, Brother Leroy Baylor Muhammad (RIP), and Brother Arthur Muhammad. Heartfelt gratitude to the Ausar Auset Society and the founder Ra Un Nefer Amen. I am grateful for the National Black Theater under the leadership of Dr. Barbara Ann Teer and Adetunde Samuel Thank you Caribbean Cultural Center African Diasporic Institute, Marta Vega, Melody Capote, Manuela Arciniegas LaSalle, and Alex LaSalle.

I am grateful for my undergraduate school passages at Hampton University (HU), where I began to establish my early identity as an educator, cultural custodian, and rites of passage practitioner. I acknowledge Dr. Alan Colon', Dr. Carlton Brown, Dr. Larnell Flannagan, Dr. Mary Christian (RIP), and Dr. Ukeles. I am grateful for the kinship that I experienced with members of the African Studies Cluster (ASC), where we were being initiated to be Jegnas, educators, healers, and keepers of our sacred knowledge, rituals, traditions, and practices. Acknowledgements to Darnell Smith, Adeeb Shabazz, Dana Oscar, Kenyatta Flemming, Adhim Deveaux, Karl Nichols, Menelik Bethea, Demetra McDonald, Demyra McDonald, Mar-Yoi Collier, Rakhunuhepp Sita (DX), Christy Robinson, La-Joi Wilson, Kaleem Caire, Lisa Caire, Nkrumah Jenings, Kareem Ahmed, Ibn Khalifah, Ishmael Muhammad, Atiba Mes Ra-Brian Anderson (RIP), Sharon Anderson (RIP),

Chris Smith, Jody Merriday, Sandra Kofa, Erica Jenkins Bryant, brothers of Kemet Nu and the sisters of Auset. Gratitude for elder and Baba Halif H. Khalifah (Owner of US and UB Books and Things across the street from HU). To some of my Hampton University brothers and friends who were not as active in the ASC – William "Bjay" Thornton, Dwayne Blythe, Kierna Mayo Smith, Denise Holt, Yvonne Orr, Carlos Walton, and Kerri Jefferies Mubaraak. I am grateful for all the powerful people who I met in the Tidewater area of Virginia. Thank you, Thomas Middleton (Norfolk State), D'Hasheem Alkebulan (Norfolk State), Nzinga Penny (Norfolk State), Keith Muhammad, and Brother George Welch (Self Improvement Education Center - Norfolk).

I acknowledge all of the following influential institutions and people who played significant roles in helping to shape my purpose, my career, and the various stages of my adult initiations: Woodlands Jr. and Sr. High School, Jay Glass (RIP), Sherri Valentine (RIP), June Sudderth (RIP), Jonathan Mosely (RIP), Tracey Woods Glover, Harambee Rites of Passage Group, Leonard "Gus" Townes, Chris Burns, Stan Ellison, David Vandiver, Jerry Franklin (RIP), Khufu Jasper, Dell . Gratitude to the Djembe Mau Society of African Ancestral Acknowledgements, Kehinde O'Uhuru, Cecil H. Parker Elementary School family, Mary Spells, Jr. High School 43 (The Study Center for Law and Peace), Dr. Kenneth Hale, Dr. LaShaune Chinnery, Carey Peyton, Anita Costa, Trace' Gaskin, Will Satterfield, Nassau Community College Liberty Partnerships Program and Gaining Early Awareness and Readiness for Undergraduate Programs, Marilyn Monroe, Adam Rogers, The Learning Tree, Sister Lois Gregory, the entire Urban Assembly Academy of History and Citizenship for Young Men (UAAHC) community, Jonathan Foy, Coalition of Schools Educating Boys of Color (COSEBOC), Ron Walker, Brenda Artwell, Deidre Farmbry, COSEBOC 444 Sankofa Passages, Ben Wright, Sankofa Facilitators, Eagle Academy Foundation, Donald Ruff, University Neighborhood Middle School (UNMS) community, Wanda Cook, Olutoju Ti Julo, Akoben Enterprise family, Elias Encarnacion, Jahlil Shabazz, Daniel Browne, Kimberly Hardy, Usson Bryant, Mahaba House family,

Nicole Sharpe, Edwina Sharpe, Imani Sharpe, Nafis Sabir, Tony Moss, Malidoma Patrice Some' (RIP), Rapha Art Life Center, Mekiel Turner Lewis, Bolo Bolo Blauweh African Drum Troupe, Lizie Bi Tra, The Hand Arts and Edutainment LLC, Kojo Ayinde Johnson, The Wake Up Everybody (WUE) Community, Shawnne Benton Gibson, the Glover family, Rich Thompson, Michael Crosswhite, Rahi Jones, Cedric Nelson, David Brown, Leonard Gill, Jennifer Safara Perry, Tina Shabazz, Nive Precil, Fabiola Didier, Vladimir Alexandre, Gail Robinson, Karen Williams, Therese Gilchrist, Christina Anderson, Patterson family, Burrowes family, Charles Rashad Pouissant, Black Brother's Day Committee, Tarra Thompson, Dr. Pedro Noguera, Sergio Argueta, Timeke Amenra-Vaughn, Charisse Boykin Browne, David Banner, Dr. Harvey Hinton, Goddard Option Center, Chad Franklin, Dare to Be King Project LLC, Dr. David Miller, and Aaron Barnette.

Additionally, I know that I may have missed someone in my acknowledgements. If you have not been mentioned and you know that you've played a significant role in my journey, please forgive me. As the saying goes, "blame it on my head, and not my heart." I am greatly appreciative of all who have sewed into my life and contributed to my passages.

Lastly, I am eternally grateful for all the boys, young men, seasoned men, and their families for trusting me to facilitate their passages. I know that you will continue to make powerful contributions to your families, community, and the planet!

ABOUT THE AUTHOR

Credit for photograph
Matthew Morgan,
Supreme Shotz

Kamau Tehuti Ptah is a luminary whose journey has intertwined conventional education with the ancient wisdom of African and Indigenous spiritual traditions. With over three decades of committed service, Kamau continues to navigate his diverse roles as a husband, Baba (father), son, brother, uncle, educator, and cultural custodian, leaving an indelible mark on the communities he serves. Receiving a Bachelor's Degree from Hampton University and a Master's Degree from Cambridge College, he has been a trailblazer in shaping transformative systems and fostering healthy cultures in educational institutions and social service agencies. As the Founder and Executive Director of Akoben Enterprise, Kamau provides culturally responsive education, professional learning, and youth development services, infusing Indigenous Spiritual ways of knowing and being to foster healing and growth primarily in communities of African, Latinx, and Indigenous heritage.

www.ingramcontent.com/pod-product-compliance
Lightning Source LLC
Chambersburg PA
CBHW061142120626
46546CB00005B/1893

* 9 7 8 1 9 5 9 8 1 1 5 8 9 *